NORTHUMBERLAND PLACE NAMES

NORTHUMBERLAND PLACE NAMES

Goodwife Hot and others

by

GODFREY WATSON

First published in Great Britain by Oriel Press in 1970.
© Godfrey Watson 1970.

Reprinted 1995, 1996 by Sandhill Press Ltd.

ISBN: 0 946098 38 7

Reprinted 2013 by Northern Heritage Services Limited.
Units 7&8 New Kennels, Blagdon Estate, Seaton Burn,
Newcastle upon Tyne, NE13 6DB
www.northern-heritage.co.uk

By kind permission of Timothy Watson.

ISBN: 978 0 9572860 6 1

Cover illustration from Thomas Moule:
'The English Counties delineated'
– map of Northumberland, 1837.

Printed in Great Britain
By Martins the Printers Ltd.
Berwick-upon-Tweed.

To Nicky

Acknowledgements

I would like to express my appreciation of the unfailing kindness shown to me by the Chief Archivist of the Northumberland Records Office and his staff, the Librarian of the Ponteland branch of the County Library and the staff of the Central Library, Newcastle upon Tyne.

Contents

Preface

Like Topsy the concept of this book just 'growed' and as it 'growed' it changed its character. For years I have been fascinated by place names. How did it come about that a village was called Ulgham or Etal? Who thought of calling their farm Whistlebare, Bakethin, Pia Troon or Pity Me?

Originally, the idea was to collect and subsequently translate, so far as possible, the more curious and entertaining names of Northumberland and more particularly of farms. But it soon became apparent that there were plenty of interesting farm names that were also the names of villages and hamlets and it seemed stupid to try and differentiate one from the other. So, whether they liked it or not, the names of all sorts of places from towns down to shepherds' huts gradually found their way into the book.

Then a problem arose. How many people would be interested in what would really amount to a dictionary of local place names—something that has been done already, though much less fully than one would wish? The great difference would be that others have generally confined themselves to names that could be traced back to medieval times while I was concerned with any, or all, of the names that appeared in any way interesting, regardless of age. Mercifully this problem solved itself because in the course of my researches—and they turned out to be far more extensive than I had ever imagined—I discovered so many interesting little bits of information, gossip and folklore that it seemed inevitable that the dictionary would grow into something very different and, I hope, more readable.

But that is not the end of the story for it is almost impossible to go on researching into place names without wanting to know not only why but how a place got its name; what was the reason for its origin; what kind of person named it and in what circumstances. This means that from its original concept of a list of derivations the book has gradually turned into an enquiry into the whole basis upon which the countryside of Northumberland has evolved.

Three books, more than any others, have been of immense assistance so far as derivations are concerned—Mawer's *Place Names of Northumberland and Durham,* Ekwall's *Oxford Dictionary of English Place Names* and *English Place Name Elements* published by the English Place Names Society. Not only have they provided between them a great many of the derivations required but, together with information derived from neighbouring counties, they have also enabled me to derive with, I hope, reasonable accuracy a number of others by association. Other derivations, and particularly those of places which do not appear in older deeds and manuscripts, have required a painstaking search for clues which has proved the most fascinating part of the whole business.

I am, of course, well aware that there are any number of people far better qualified than I to attempt a book of this sort. My excuse for taking it upon myself is that no one else seems to have done it. Yet the need really is urgent for farms are being absorbed in, or combined with, others while names in general alter their spelling, let alone their pronunciation. The Bog becomes Brownchester, the Vicarage Farm becomes The Venture, Dinnington Colliery blossoms forth as Brunswick, Woolsington tends to alter to Wolsington and a building estate absorbs Heathery Shank. As the years pass the task will therefore become not easier but more difficult.

The effort, though infinitely rewarding, has, of course, been a complicated one. Anyone who has tried to decipher the handwriting of a relative, let alone that of a medieval scribe, must appreciate the difficulty of accurate transcription. No wonder that The Hermitage becomes Tharmitag in more than one document and The Hall Barns appears at least once as Thawle Barnys while Coastley during a single century (the thirteenth) was spelt Cotisley and Cocelay.

Quite apart from the inevitable errors in transcription, it was only in the last century or so that any effort seems to have been made to standardise spelling. Shakespeare is supposed to have signed his name in over fifty different ways and one of the Loraines of Kirkharle, in making her will, spelt her name (or rather that of the relatives to whom she was making bequests) in three different ways in consecutive lines. It is hardly surprising, therefore, that even the greatest experts get their derivations wrong. Indeed they differ radically over many Northumbrian names and where this is the case I have just had to select the most likely answer.

It was high time, also, that someone made an effort to discourage by substituting more accurate information, the woefully misguided efforts that have been made to derive place names from whatever seemed handiest. It really will not do to say that Akeld is a corruption of 'all-killed' because it is near Homildon Hill, when the name had already existed for centuries before the battle was fought. But even this is preferable to explaining Amerside as 'Lovers' Walk' on the strength of *amo* being Latin for 'I love' or to employ German and Greek, as was attempted by early historians.

Where there are authorities to whom recourse can be made, and where these authorities disagree, I have normally chosen the most modern for the simple reason that the art of deriving place names has been advanced tremendously during the present century, particularly by the Scandinavians who seem to understand our language better than we do ourselves. Everything else being equal, I have chosen the topographical explanation rather than the personal. For instance Mawer tends to fall back distressingly often on 'Eggleswiggle's homestead' where Ekwall gives 'the farm by the oak tree' or something of that sort: they cannot both be right, which I find comforting (if somewhat confusing). Furthermore, an enormous number of place names had already been corrupted in some way before they ever appeared in writing. When I err, therefore, it will be in good company.

Indeed it is sometimes very difficult to choose between two inter pretations which seem, on the evidence, to be equally likely but in respect of which no definition has hitherto been attempted. Where the name may be derived from the position of the hamlet or farm it is clearly possible to examine the location either on the Ordnance map or, better still, on the ground. Even these methods of proof can be deceptive for there must be any number of farmsteads that, like Brockdam and Espershields, have moved quite a distance from their

original situation. On the other hand to be guided by the pronuncia
tion is a great deal safer than to place one's trust in the spelling, even
where the latter may be reasonably consistent. It is an important
feature of the Northumbrian dialect that it is nearer, both in the
words used and their pronunciation, to that of our Germanic ancestors than any other speech in the country—in fact we have virtually
become the guardians of the old tongue.

It must be obvious that place names reflect, according to their
antiquity and other factors, the language of the different races who
have occupied the countryside throughout the ages. One has inevitably to decide what to call these different races, or rather the language
that they spoke. For the sake of simplicity this book makes no effort
to differentiate between Welsh and Gaelic but refers merely to Celtic.
Likewise the language of our Anglian forefathers is referred to as
Old English, while Norse and Danish appear simply as Scandinavian.

A further choice had to be made. Should one set out each derivation in full with a note of the original words from which each part
of the name originated, together with the different stages of evolution
between ancient and modern? Or should one skip the intermediate
stages and state flatly what the meaning appears to be? Except
where there appears to be good reason to the contrary, the second
course has been chosen. In other words, in this as in all other respects,
the author's principal aim has been to produce a book which all who
may be interested can read, rather than a work of reference.

Again for the sake of clarity I have made little effort to guess at the
finer meaning of many of the words that our ancestors used. For
instance such words as Ham, Tun, Worth and Wic have borne at
different times almost infinite shades of meaning. If there is anything
definite, however, about them it is that they were at any rate used to
differentiate from each other. It seemed reasonable, therefore, if not
strictly accurate, to describe them in every case as Village, Homestead,
Enclosure and Farm and to leave it at that.

Finally it must be acknowledged that there remain far too many
names of farms in Northumberland, if not of hamlets and villages,
for which no rational explanation is forthcoming, though educated
guesswork is of course possible. I wonder if it is too much to hope
that anyone reading this book and having any knowledge to impart

or corrections to suggest, will come forward with what information they have and will write to me at Prestwick Whins, Ponteland, Northumberland?

Note: Godfrey Watson sadly died in 1976.

CHAPTER 1

THREE thousand years ago Northumberland, like the rest of England, was one great forest, principally of oak and ash, broken only by expanses of hill and moor and by swamps that have subsequently been drained. During the Bronze Age the whole population of the county was probably no more than a few hundreds. There was plenty of land to go round and no particular reason why those who settled in the country should not find all they wanted further south. Even in the Iron Age of the Celts who preceded the Roman invasions, the population of all England, let alone Northumberland, as we know it, would only have been something like half a million.

The Bronze-agers had been largely, if not entirely, wanderers who grazed their animals in forest clearings and on the lower fringes of the moors, and then moved on. It was, therefore, not until Celtic times that habitations became sufficiently permanent to acquire names of their own. This was the dawn of agriculture in Northumberland, as elsewhere, for the Celts, being tillers of the soil, required a fixed base from which to operate and this in turn meant choosing a spot where there was not only dry ground but water and shelter from the wind. Above all the soil must be light and easily worked for wheeled ploughs were only just coming in and the means of cultivation were in general too primitive to allow of any of the heavier soils being tackled.

These people, therefore, began at the top and very gradually worked down the hills, increasing the size of their clearings as they went. What particularly concerns us here is the importance of the forest in the economy of these earlier inhabitants and for centuries to come. Only by hacking it away tree by tree or, where it was safe to do so, burning the timber where it stood, could a better living be scratched from the soil. The only alternative, indeed, was to venture out on to the edge of the moorland in places where, though less fertile, the soil could be worked without the back-breaking labour of clearing the forest. In any case it was necessary that the newly won land should be enclosed as soon as possible, not so much to mark it off from the neighbours—the forest effectively did that—as to keep out wild animals and to keep in the stock that these new agriculturists tended. This enclosure could be effected either by rough timber fencing, by palisades or, more commonly by digging a ditch and throwing up a bank—the 'dic' or dyke of our Anglian forefathers yet to come. Such dykes were also used to mark the boundaries of the chieftains' estates and, on a larger scale still, as defences against aggression from 'foreigners'.

As yet there were no towns, not even villages: just tiny hamlets and isolated farms, but with the Celts had come the first place names that we know of, and the basis of so many thousands more to come, which would describe not only the geographical location of a place in terms of hill, valley and stream but, in particular, of clearing and enclosure. Henceforward it was to be 'somebody's clearing', 'the clearing on the hill', 'the enclosure by the stream' and so forth, with every kind of variation but little originality.

> *On Keilderside, the wind blows wide,*
> *There sounds nae hunting horn*
> *That rings so sweet as the winds that beat*
> *Round banks where Tyne is born.*

So runs one of the loveliest verses of 'A Jacobite's Exile' by Swinburne and it introduces us to one of the few purely Celtic names still to be found in Northumberland. It is from the Kielder Burn that the village of *Kielder* takes its name, and it means Violent Water.

It might be thought that *Pity Me*, not far from the Roman Dere Street that runs through Corbridge to the Border, was one of those fancy names that have been given to farms in the last couple of hundred years or so. It is nothing of the kind, but a corruption of two Celtic words meaning the Field of the Graves. No great imagination is required to picture the struggle, perhaps the last struggle, of the Britons against the Roman invaders steadily pushing their way northwards.

Painshaw, and probably *Painshawfield* as well, owe their name to a Rocky Summit; *Powtreuet* (in 1315 Poltrerneth) to the Homestead by the Slow-moving Stream and *Plenmellor* the Top of a Bare Hill. All of them are Celtic in origin, as are those that follow.

When we approach the *Cheviots*—a name so old that no one seems to know what it means—we also begin to approach history as we know it. *Mindrum* signifies a Mountain Ridge, and *Canno Mill*, near Kirknewton, takes its name from 'canu', the Celtic word for a Hill; neither of them very surprising. *Old Yeavering*, however, has a history out of all proportion to its present size. The name itself is a corruption of Gefrin, denoting the presence of Goats, and a shepherd's hut now marks the spot where one of the palaces of the ancient Kings of Northumbria stood. Bede wrote about two of these secondary palaces, calling them Ad Gefrin and Ad Murum, the second of which we shall meet again on the Roman Wall. It was at the first—in other words at Yeavering—that King Edwin is thought to have been baptised by Paulinus, with far reaching results. *Yeavering Bell* moreover, and the surrounding hills, had previously been a favourite haunt of King Arthur, or so it is said, and the scene of a famous victory over the invading English.

Returning to the west of the county, into the remoter valleys of which the ancient inhabitants would seem to have been forced, there appear *Glenwhelt*, the Wild Valley, and *Glendue*, the Black or Dark Valley. Then in the parish of Simonburn there are two places whose names are clearly of Celtic origin but which have so far defied all efforts to translate them. One is *Tecket*, which may conceivably be connected with a beacon on the neighbouring hill and the other is *Teppermoor*. The name of another place, *Farglow*, near Thirlwall, was once thought to be 'the picturesque perversion of some Celtic name' but has proved to be nothing of the kind. In 1279 it appears as Farglew and there is good reason to think that it means a Spot where Bull-baiting took place.

Watch Trees, near Coanwood, is like Pity Me to the extent that the name sounds so innocent (and so modern) while in fact it is quite complicated (and very old). The first word is in fact a corruption of two Celtic words meaning Lower Wood and the second has of course been added in ignorance.

Only two names from this period seem to have survived along the coast. One is *Ross* which simply means a Promontory and the second is *Cambois*. The latter is interesting because it proves so neatly the point that, in this matter of derivations, you can never trust the spelling while you can very often trust the pronunciation, because our language has been handed on almost entirely by word of mouth. No amount of frenchifying by Norman clerks has succeeded in changing the pronunciation of this name from the original Camus, meaning something crooked; in this case a Bay.

Troughend, near Otterburn, the home of the Reeds for so many hundreds of years appears in the history of the thirteenth and fourteenth centuries as Trequenne, Torquen and finally Troghwen. The Laird of Troghwen, as he was known, sounds to our ears much more romantic than the Squire of Troughend but the origin of the name remains obscure save that, once more, it is almost certainly Celtic. Indeed Redesdale and the adjoining countryside show quite a few traces of the Celts. *Carrycoats*, for instance, comes from Caer-y-coed, the Stronghold in the Woods. *Comogan*, also near *Birtley* (the Bright Clearing) is reputed to be a corruption of Come-an-gan, implying a hospitable place where there is a good store of everything. This idea of 'Cut-and-come-again' may be attractive but it is a great deal more likely that the real answer is Caer-Mogon, the Stronghold of the god Mogon, the local deity that the Romans invoked to protect their advanced station at Habitancum (Risingham). This is all the more probable because of the seven neighbouring Celtic camps or Caeraw (hill fortresses).

The first of them is at *Carry House* which probably means exactly that (Caeraw). Then come *Goodwife Hot* and *Garret Hot*. Who the lady in question was, history does not relate and one suspects Goodwife of being a corruption from the Celtic: like Old Wife, however, it may have been a later description of the Goddess of Fertility. Certainly the second is Caer-yt-holt, the Fort (or Castle) on the Hill.

Countess Park is named after one of the many Celtic variants for a Hill, and *Mill Knock* is the Millstone Hillock. Then come two more names of later origin; the first being *Buteland*—that is to say Bota's Land. In the case of the second, the remains of the Sunken Enclosures or Hut-circles that originally sheltered humans have since been used throughout the ages to protect animals; hence the Middle English name of *Nightfolds*. Not so far away is *Catreen*; surely the old Stronghold on the Promontory? An example of the same period in another part of the country is *Pennywells*, in Hulne Park which rather surprisingly derives its name from Pen-y-gwel, the Rampart on the Hill.

It will be seen from the derivation of several of these names that our English ancestors sometimes took an existing Celtic name and, either because they did not understand its meaning or because they needed to amplify it, added something of their own. An outstanding example of this is *Kirkley* which had nothing to do with a church but was originally named Cruc; yet another word for a Hill. To this was later added the English 'hlaw', also meaning a Hill. The explanation, as in some other cases, is presumably that the place had been known for so long as Kirk, or something of the sort, that its original meaning was forgotten. *Kirkhill* and *Kirksyde*, nearby, are of much later date but the derivation is in fact the same.

High Carrick, near Elsdon, is another place that rejoices in a bilingual name for it is the Old English Dwelling (or Farm) by the Celtic Fort (or Stronghold). By the same token *Dunterley* in North Tynedale owes its name to the Celtic 'dintref' or Village by the Castle and 'leah', the Old English for a clearing.

It seems strange that so few traces of the old culture should have survived in Northumbrian place names and there are, one supposes, two reasons. The first lies in the more open nature of much of the county compared to, say, Cumberland and the second (hypothetically) in the better fighting qualities of the Anglian tribes in question compared to those of other invaders. It must be conceded, however, that this is not a very convincing argument, considering the extent to which these particular Celts must have been Romanised and their equipment correspondingly improved. The real answer may very well lie in the feuds that divided them and the constant struggle that they had to wage with their brethren from north of what is now the Border.

It must be acknowledged, also, that many of the place names to be dealt with later, which cannot easily be explained in any other way, may very well contain Celtic elements which are now impossible to trace.

CHAPTER 2

IT is a curious fact that although, militarily speaking, the Romans had more to do with Northumberland than almost any other part of the country, there are precious few signs to be found of their influence on the civilian population. Furthermore their military camps, roads and depots, although well known to us today by name as well as on the ground, have had still less effect on the place names of the county.

No one seems to know of any Roman villas or estates in the North, such as are to be found elsewhere, and what farms were created must have fallen into disuse until in medieval times the increase in population caused these 'Old Lands' (as they were called) to be brought into cultivation again. The square Celtic fields of an acre or less, painfully won from forest or moor and immediately enclosed, remained much as they were.

The great difference that the Romans made in the countryside lay in the roads that they drove through it in as near as possible a straight line. Before this there had been nothing but the prehistoric tracks that had kept to the higher, open, ground. Now the heavier, and more fertile, soils were rendered not only more accessible but also capable of cultivation by the improved ploughs that the Romans introduced.

In point of fact only one place name, that of *Corbridge* bears any resemblance to the Roman original. It describes the Bridge over the Cor Burn and one can only suppose the latter to have been named after Corstopitum—or was the reverse in fact the case?

All this, of course, serves to introduce once more the subject of 'camps'. Generally speaking, the word 'camp' in a Northumbrian place name denotes the presence of a Celtic or prehistoric settlement. Thus *Campfield* at Cornhill, which was earlier known as Camp Hill, is near earthworks that are in fact remains of ancient dwellings. The same applies to *Camp House* near Whalton (near which are the Earthworks called the Dead Men's Graves) to *Camp House* at Matfen, *Camp Hill* at Colwell (near Pity Me Camp) and *Camp Houses* near Norham.

Campville was once Lenterencleugh—the Ravine where there was a look-out place in which a Lantern could be hung to warn Coquet-dale of Scottish raids. Subsequently the name became Lanternside and then, in the early nineteenth century the owner, struck by the 'fine remains of a strong British camp' on the farm, changed its name to the present one. Surely he could have done better?

On the other hand, *Camp Hill*, just north of Berwick, marks the spot where the English camped before the battle of Halidon Hill while *Encampment* is where the Scots spent the night after capturing Ford Castle and before giving battle at Flodden.

But all this is a far cry from the Romans, the remains of whose forts and dwellings are so often commemorated by the word Chester (the modern equivalent of the Old English Ceaster which in turn was derived from the Latin Castra, a Camp). *Rudchester*, known to the Romans as Vindobala, appears in 1250 as Rucestre. There are several different theories explaining how the place got its name: all are plausible and the whole thing only goes to show how difficult it sometimes is to be positive about a derivation. All agree, of course, that the second part of the word signifies a Roman Fort but one claims that it was Rudda's, another that it was the Red One's (quite possibly the same thing) and a third that it was the Red Fort, so called because at one time there must have been a fire, for reddened stones have been dug up there. A fourth, and probably the most likely theory, is that this was the Rough Camp.

Funnily enough (or is there a connection?) Rudchester was owned for many years by the Rutherfords, one of whom fought in the Civil War, an account of which ensured his imperishable fame (and one would hope that of his wife who, rather unfairly, remains unsung). 'Here must not be omitted', it reads, 'that memorable Gentleman Volunteer M. Gawen Rutherford who, though he was not slain in the service, yet deserves to be had in perpetual remembrance for his loyalty for having had 29 children by one wife'. Some say he had thirty but apparently his loyalty lay not so much in begetting a whole platoon as in the fact that no less than nineteen of his sons were killed in the war. As a matter of fact this was not the first time in history that a Rutherford of Rudchester has displayed his martial spirit for was there not one,

> *A hot and haughty Rutherford,*
> *Men called him Dickon-draw-the-sword.*

A variation of the name, which is almost certainly in this case the Rough Camp, is to be found in *Ruchester*, near Chollerford. An apparently near relation is *Rochester*, once the Roman Bremenium but now the Camp frequented by Rooks.

Chesterwood is really Chesterworth, the Enclosure or Farm by the Camp! *Chesterholm* the Flats by the Burn near the Roman Vindolanda and *Chesterhope* the Blind Valley near Habitancum. *Gilchester* near Stamfordham was once known as Gripchester, thus introducing the word 'grip' for a Ditch, which still survives in the grip, or channel, of a cowbyre, so that the farm is really the Camp by the Ditch. *Hedchester Law*, not so far away, is the Camp covered with Heather while *Hetchester* was once known as Haycestre—either the Camp where Hay is now made or (perhaps more likely) the Camp enclosed by a Hedge.

It is sometimes difficult to tell after the lapse of so much time whether a particular Chester is in fact of Roman origin or not. The ancestry of *Raechester*, for instance, which is the Camp in the Corner or Bend (of the burn), *Ferney Chesters* (the Camp grown over with Bracken) and *Greenchesters*, where the Scots bivouaced before the battle of Otterburn, may possibly be even more ancient than those already mentioned.

On the other hand *Whitchester* is undoubtedly the White (or Dry) expanse by the Roman Camp and *Outchester* is the Roman Camp frequented by Owls; *Chester Hill* taking its name from the same place. *Chesters Farm*, not far away, has probably an identical origin while *Chesters*, near Chollerford is, of course, named after the biggest Roman fort in the county (Cilurnum) which covers nearly six acres. Subsequently the place was known as Scytlescester, the Camp that was Barred or Fenced in (probably as a Cattle fold).

At *Gloster Hill*, near Amble, a Roman altar was discovered in 1856 and there are other signs of Roman occupation: hence the name Gloucestre in 1178. The better known Gloucester, in the county of that name, derives its name from 'ceaster' and from the Celtic word for Bright or Splendid. In the case of Gloster Hill it is just possible that the name is a corruption of Goatchester, the Goats being the Marshy land by the Gildean burn where salt used to be made.

Gloucester Lodge, near Earsdon, however, has a very different connection, being named (or perhaps re-named) after Prince William of Gloucester who commanded the Volunteer Corps at Hartley during the invasion scare of 1795.

But all camps did not necessarily become Chesters: some of them have blossomed forth as Castles, as in the case of *Roughcastle* which betrays its probable origin by its very Roughness. Then there is *Horncastle* which owes its name not to the Herons, its one-time owners, so much as its position on a Horn or Tongue of land between the Wansbeck and the Ray Burn. In 1765 the place was described as a 'poor thatched building' that was not far from ancient earthworks. *Horncliffe* and *Hornestead* similarly represent a Cliff and a Steading (respectively) standing on a Tongue of Land.

It might reasonably be thought that *Ted Castle* described some old timer's stronghold but again it is an old Camp that gives the place its name, and Tadda was the Settler who came to live there.

It is not particularly surprising that Hadrian's Wall has lent its name to a number of places, considering its claim to be the most important landmark in the county. Indeed not only is it a landmark but (unfortunately) the source of stone for an uncounted number of buildings. It is not surprising therefore to find in the ceiling of the crypt in Hexham Abbey, which dates back to the seventh century, a stone commemorating two Roman Emperors who jointly ruled the Empire until one, having caused the other's death, decreed that his name should be struck from all inscriptions, including this.

Wall, therefore means precisely what it says, while *Wall Houses* refers to the ruined buildings that preceded the present hamlet, in the same way that *Housesteads* denotes the (Farm) Steading where the Houses, that is to say the remains of the Roman Fort of Borcovi-cium, had been. In the north of the county stands a farm which is known as *Housedon Haugh*, the Low-lying Ground by the Hill where stood a 'House' (in other words an Old Building), and is the subject of one of Robert Story's poems that recalls his youth as a shepherd:

> *Pours the spring its earliest green*
> *Upon Hoseden still?*
> *Are the milk-white hawthorns seen*
> *Upon Hoseden still?*

Wallsend (or Segedunum as the Romans called it) requires no explanation, *Benwell* means Within the Wall, and that brings us to *Walbottle*. This, the 'botle', Building or, in this case, Palace on the Wall is almost certainly the Ad Murum described by Bede as being one of the residences of the ancient Kings of Northumbria.

Heddon-on-the-Wall is the Hill covered with Heather, just as *Black Heddon* is the Black or Gloomy Hill where nothing but Heather grows. Yet *East Heddon*, practically adjoining Heddon-on-the-Wall, is derived completely differently. It is Hidda's Pasture or 'winn', a variation of the word used by the Vikings when they named America Vinland, and provides an excellent example of the corruption of a name to agree with what people think it should be.

It is not surprising to find that *Walwick* denotes the Farm by the Wall, nor that *Walltown* is the Homestead in a like situation. It was from this, one of the ancestral homes of the Ridleys of Tynedale, that Bishop Ridley wrote his last letter bidding 'farewell, my beloved brother, John Ridley of the Walltown' before being burnt at the stake.

Now when our English forefathers conquered the Celtish tribes they did not drive them completely out of what is now Northumberland. Those that were left in evidence were almost invariably known as Wealh or Weala; a name that was perpetuated in Wallis, Wallace and the like and that described a 'Welshman' or, if you prefer it, an Aborigine. *Wallish Walls*, for instance, describes the Foundations of an older structure now inhabited by a Welshman. (In the seventeenth century it was known as Twoe Walliges.) In the same way the name *Wally Thorn* probably represents the place by the Thorntree, and *Wallridge* the Ridge where a Welshman lived.

Another of the same kind is commemorated in 'Show me the way to Wallington', the song that begins so improbably 'Dear Billy Sam' and continues

> *show me the way to Wallington;*
> *I have a grey mare o' my ain, she nier gies ower gallopin';*
> *Down by Bingfield Kame, and by the banks of Hallington,*
> *Through by Bavington Syke—and that's the way to Wallington.*

Wallington means, quite simply, the Homestead of the Welshman's (or by inference the Heathen's) People, just as *Bingfield* means the Expanse (that is to say, something larger than a clearing) inhabited by Bynna's People. Kame, meaning a Ridge, we shall meet again later.

A 'sike' which appears over and over again in the place names of Northumberland, has never changed its meaning from a Small Stream or Rivulet. *Bavington* is the Homestead of Babba's People but Hallington presents certain difficulties.

When General Wade was required to move his army from the East Coast to the West in order to deal with the 'Rebellion' of 1745 he soon discovered that it was impossible to move his artillery and stores over what passed at that time as a road. A new highway was subsequently made, using the stones of the Roman Wall as a foundation. Hence the 'Military Road'. By the side of this road, Roman, Military or whatever you may like to call it, just before it plunges westward to cross the Tyne at Chollerford, stands a plain cross commemorating the battle of *Heavenfield*. Here, not far from *St Oswald's Hill Head* the Christian King Oswald defeated the heathen Mercians under Cadwallon in one of the great battles of Northumbria; Cadwallon himself being pursued and finally killed at Dennisburn. Where this latter place was is not known exactly but there is evidence that it may have been on what is now known as the Rowley Burn, where it enters the Devil's Water.

Now Leland, writing in the sixteenth century, says 'there is a fame that Oswald won the battle at Halydene a two miles est from St Oswald's Ashe and that Haliden is it that Bede caulith Havenfield'. This would place 'Haliden' somewhat east of *Hazeldean*, which used to be known as Knitell-hasell or Cnytel's Hazelbush, and now the Hazel Valley. What then is the modern name for Haliden? The accepted answer is *Hallington*, several miles to the north of the accepted site of the battle. Admittedly Hallington was known in 1247 as Halidene (The Holy Valley) but confusion is made worse by William Waiken of Haliden having 'rights in the pasture of Hallington' as if they were two different places.

But all this is a far cry from the Romans. Perhaps it is some excuse that it is in a Roman altar that the modern cross commemorating the battle stands.

CHAPTER 3

WHEN the Romans were forced by events at home to retire from Britain the military, if not the political, position in which they left the Celtic inhabitants must have been very much like that in which the newly independent countries of the mid-twentieth century find themselves. The natives, even where they had not inter-married with the men from Spain, Holland and the Balkans who were loosely known as Romans, had been extensively Romanised. They were infinitely more cultured than before but considerably less warlike for they had allowed their conquerors to do the bulk of the fighting against the Picts and Caledonians to the north. Despite all the efforts of Severus and others to destroy these Borderers of the fourth and fifth centuries A.D. they succeeded in doing nothing of the sort. Bitterly the Romans accused the Caledonians of spending their days immersed up to the neck in the mosses of their native land and then popping up again to harry their would-be conquerors.

When the British (to differentiate them from the other Celtic tribes) were left to their own devices they were not only fair game for those same neighbours but made things worse by continually warring among themselves. And so began the Dark Ages during which orderly government disappeared and with it the culture that order had made possible. As a result it is unlikely that many records of what went on during the next few centuries were kept, and certainly very few have survived. In fact we have little knowledge of what transpired.

What we do know is that, during this period, Britain as a whole was subjected to an ever increasing number of raids by Jutes, Angles, Saxons and Friesians, to be followed in more historical times by Norsemen and Danes. The plight of the Romanised Celtic inhabitants was worse in the north of England than elsewhere for they were

28

sandwiched between these invaders from overseas and those from the north—that is to say the aforesaid Picts and Caledonians, to say nothing of those more recent arrivals from Ireland, the Scots.

Apart from the preliminary reconnaissance, these invasions took the form of emigrations rather than of purely military raids for, like the Pilgrim Fathers, the invaders brought with them their wives and families. All that part of the East Coast from the Humber up to the Forth was settled by the Angles, that is to say, a number of tribes from what we now know as Schleswig Holstein. After some pretty fierce fighting with the Celtic tribes, the first Anglian villages began to appear. Some, like *Stamfordham*, originally the Homestead by the Stony Ford, grew up round a village green which was surrounded not only by the mud-and-timber huts of the settlers but by a palisade inside which domestic animals could be driven at night. Other settlements just straggled along a track or the bank of the stream which was an essential feature of the place.

At first these habitations would take the form of a Homestead, Hamlet or 'tun' consisting of a few huts inhabited by families connected by blood. Later on they might grow into 'hams' or villages proper. Thus when the village of *Ovingham* (that is to say, of Ofa's people) outgrew its surroundings, the Ovingas started up a fresh Homestead of *Ovington*.

Very often these settlements were named after the family, or followers, of the pioneer who originally settled there. In other ways, also, it must have been very much like the colonisation of North America. There was the same necessity to carve a farm out of the primeval forest, the same struggle against the local inhabitants and the same problem of trapping and growing enough food to keep the community alive.

And so these early founding fathers were immortalised; the followers of Eadlac by *Acklington*, Cifa by *Chevington*, Ceabba by *Choppington*, Ida by *Edington*, Grotta by *Grotington*, Tytel by *Titlington*. Despite the fact that *Tritlington* appears in a sixteenth-century document as Fricklington, it owes its origin to a settler called Tyrhtel just as *Widdrington* was founded by Wudhere, *Willington* by Wifel, *Woolsington* by Wulfrige and *Yetlington* by Geatela. These are only some of the places whose names commemorate the family

Homestead. We shall come across others later.

Then, of course, there are the people who were known not by the name of their leader so much as the kind of place from which they came. Thus *Shilvington* is the Homestead founded by the People living on a Shelf of land by the river, *Melkington* by those (most probably) who dwelt by a Rich Milky Pasture, *Felkington* from a Faeg Ness or Multi-coloured Hill, *Riplington* by those from a Ridge and *Dinnington* just from a Hill. In the same way it was the People from the Erring (or Bright) Burn who gave their name to *Errington*. Lastly there is *Doddington* (or Dorrington as for some obscure reason it used to be known). It is conceivable that it was Dodda's People who gave it its name but much more likely that its founders came from *Dod Law*, the Rounded or Polled Hill, nearby. It is no accident that the naturally polled Aberdeen Angus cattle are known in the Borders as Doddies, nor that *Dodley* near Harlow Hill, lies on a Rounded Hillside.

Easington, the Homestead of the People living on the Yese (an Old Celtic stream name which is a variant of Ouse) is worth a paragraph to itself if only because *Easington Grange* was described in 1875 in an advertisement that included the following panegyric, '... the very ne-plus-ultra of turnip and barley soils, seated in the perfume of bean and clover blossoms at the elbow of that ancient and erudite chair of agriculture, Belford ... For utility and ornament ... the prophetic mind beholds in all these the future 'Cirencester' of Northumberland, inculcating other ethics than the childish invention of parliamentary crutches for the tottering steps of the infant farmer'. The *Pall Mall Gazette*, commenting on this advertisement, speculated at some length on what this seat of learning actually consisted of and went on to remark with some justification that 'ordinary men would seem out of place in such a spot'.

There are, however, a few place names which are now indistinguishable from these but originally referred to a 'dun' or Hill. Thus *Bassington* is the Hill occupied by that far-flung and important clan the Bassingas, and *Berrington* the Hill of Bere's People, the same clan that colonised *Berryburn* and *Berryhill*.

The honour of bearing the oldest English name in Northumberland may well go to *Birling* near Warkworth, which was probably founded in the sixth century. As late as 1187 it was still known as Berlinga, meaning Of the Sons of the Cupbearer or perhaps, less romantically, of the man whose shield bore the device of a Boar.

Great Whittington, founded by Hwita's People, has been known for the greater part of its existence as Muckle Whittington and, in consequence, was thought for long enough to be the place where Oswulf, one of the many kings of Northumbria to be murdered, met his death in 759. But the delightfully named Mechil Wongtune mentioned in the Life of St Cuthbert, with which it has been confused, was actually Medil Wong Tun, the Town of General Assembly, subsequently known as Medelmost Medelton and now just as *Middleton*, near Wooler.

The name, Middleton, of course, usually denotes the Middle of three or more Homesteads, just as *Middlepart* commemorates the sale of the Shortflatt estate in three portions in 1690. *Middleton*, near Belsay, used to be known as Middleton Morell and is thought to have belonged at one time to King Malcolm of Scotland. It was named, however, after the man who was kinsman and steward to Robert Mowbray, the Earl of Northumberland (of whose connection with Bamburgh we will hear later) and who lived at another Homestead nearby, namely *Morleston*.

Such an estate as this would have been bounded in its earliest days by banks of earth known as dykes, along which might run 'here-paths', that is to say paths along which an Army could pass. This word 'here' appears in several of our place names and was originally thought to signify an army in more instances than has subsequently proved to be the case. One of the few names for which this interpretation appears certain is *Harbottle*, the Army Building(s) or Barracks, and the origin, funnily enough, of the surname Arbuckle which, although conspicuous by its almost entire absence in Northumberland, has spread as far afield as America. Another is *Harehaugh*, near Rothbury, which represents the Low-lying Ground near the river where stood an Old English Fort. *Harlow Hill*, on the other hand describes the Hill where the People assembled; the word 'here' denoting any kind of multitude, military or otherwise. *Harlow Bower*, near Whitfield, signifies in the same way the Cottage or Retreat by the Assembly Hill.

Confusion becomes worse confounded when one examines some of the other Northumbrian names beginning with Har. The Old English word 'har' meant Hoary or Grey and was applied in particular to stones and thence to the stones which were used so extensively to mark the boundaries between one estate and another. This is the explanation of another *Harehaugh* (this time near Bellingham) where a Boundary stone could be seen until quite recently. *Harwood* is the Wood that marks the Boundary between the baronies of Hartburn and Redesdale, and *Harwood Shiel* the Summer Hut by the Wood marking the Boundary between Shotley High Quarter and Hexhamshire High Quarter. In the same way another Valley, where there was a Boundary Stone, was known as Harestanden and finally as *Harsondale*.

Nevertheless 'har' could in some cases be grey (or more accurately, hoary) without bearing any secondary meaning, *Harecross* for instance having started out as Hare Hill (or the Hawe Hill) while *Hareshaw* is the Grey Wood and *Harewalls* the Grey Walls. Yet *Harelaw* and *Haredene* are the Hill and Valley respectively where Hares are frequently to be seen.

It is all very confusing and it is made no less so by the obtrusion of two more names quite differently derived. *Great Hardish*, for instance, may well have been a Parklike enclosure where a Herd was kept while *Harsley* is probably the Clearing among the Hazels.

As has already been indicated, boundary marks were once an important feature of the countryside for there came into being many areas of 'debatable lands' where disputes were frequent and not always easily settled. Thus *Threepit Hill* is the Disputed Hill and *Threepwood* the Disputed Wood. *Bounder House* marks the boundary between the manors of Capheaton and Belsay and *Bounderlands* that between the baronies of Langley and Wark.

Generally speaking, however, these disputes did not become an important fact in people's lives until many years after the Conquest for it was not until some time in the thirteenth century that the countryside became widely settled. Until then only the better land would have been taken up and there would be plenty of forest and marsh intervening.

CHAPTER 4

WITH *Cartington,* the Homestead of Kiartan's People, and with *Carterside,* the Hillside where someone of the same name probably settled, we enter on a new era—that of the Viking raids carried out by the Norsemen and Danes. To begin with, these were separate ventures by distinct peoples and the main source of annoyance was the Danes—particularly under Halfden. The principal result, however, was the harassing of the coastal villages and particularly of the unfortunate inhabitants of the Monasteries at Lindisfarne and Tynemouth.

During this period, in fact, perhaps because the Northern Angles were better fighters than their Anglian and Saxon cousins; perhaps because the countryside was not so attractive to the invaders, Scandinavian influence seems at first to have been inconsiderable. Elsewhere, the East Coast bristles with Danish names; the North and East Ridings of Yorkshire, for instance, boasting any number of places whose names end in 'by' and 'thorpe'. On the West Coast the names are different again with 'scale', 'thwaite' and 'beck' showing just as clearly that Cumberland and Westmorland were settled by Norsemen.

Later on, various treaties seem to have been made by the inhabitants of what is today broadly speaking Northumberland with the United Scandinavian kingdom. Gradually, and without undue bloodshed, the Scandinavian influence grew until it was virtually paramount. The consequence of this comparatively peaceful assimilation has been that our speech has been very considerably influenced by Scandinavian words but our place names very little, apart from a few such as *Byker,* the Marsh by the Village. Yet there is one part of the county, in particular, that shows signs of a concentration of

Scandinavian settlers, namely Coquetdale, or rather the countryside round Hrotha's Stronghold—the *Rothbury* of today.

Hrotha himself was English but there are several place names hereabouts that are partly or entirely Scandinavian. Some like Cartington and *Plainfield* have been anglicised. The latter name for instance, denoting an Expanse of land shaped like an Arrow, ends with the Old English 'feld' meaning a piece of Open Country that is more extensive than a Clearing. Yet it begins with the Scandinavian word 'fleinn' and indeed as recently as 1572 the place was known as Flaynefeld.

Nevertheless there are names in the Rothbury District, as nowhere else in Northumberland, that are completely Scandinavian. One such is *Trewhitt*, meaning the Clearing among the Fir (or Pine) trees: yet *Trewitley* not so very many miles away has always had an English ending. Once it was Tyrwytschel, denoting a Shieling or Summer Hut in the Fir clearing: then from ignorance of the original meaning it acquired the Old English ending 'leah', meaning once more a Clearing.

When the Vikings discovered America in the eleventh century they christened it Vinland—the Meadow land. The same word 'vin' is alleged to appear in *Tosson*, giving it the authentically Scandinavian, but mildly improbable, meaning of Flax Meadow. It is only fair to add that the name may equally have described in Old English a Stone marking a Look-out place.

Another name which lends itself to almost unlimited argument is *Snitter*. Standing, as it does, on the very point of a narrow ridge, both possible explanations could hold water. The first is that the name is derived from the Middle English 'sniteren', meaning to Snow, but the second brings in the Scandinavian word for a Corner of land. If the former is correct the place has an affinity with *The Snods* (or Snowy Place) in the extreme south of the county.

Apart from *Blindburn*, which takes its name from the Foaming Stream, almost all the remaining names in the county that have Scandinavian associations contain the name of the original settler allied to an Old English word describing the place. Thus *Amerston* is Eymundr's Homestead and *Amerside* probably his Hillside. *Balkwell* denotes the Spring where Balki lived, *Boltshope* the Blind Valley of

Bolti and *Brotherwick*, Brodr's Farm. The Village of Haltor's people is now known as *Eltringham* and Freywith's Summer Hut(s) as *Farrow Shields*.

Nubbock has always presented a bit of a problem, so far as its name is concerned. In 1608 it was described as 'Yokesley or Nubbock' and earlier still as Jakele and as Yorkesland. Originally it must have been Iokell's Clearing but the only clue to the present name is to be found in a document of 1717 which refers to 'Yokeley alias Nub-bock alias Nobbydykes'. It rather looks, then, as if the place was finally named after the Undulating nature of the Banks that enclosed it.

Other Scandinavians to leave their mark were Gagni and Kjarni, whose Hills are known respectively as *Gainslaw* and *Kearsley*. And, of course, Sveinn (a name only too well known to students of history round the time of the Conquest as Swayn) whose Homestead was at *Swainston*.

Then there is that romantic gentleman the Nattfari, or Traveller by Night, who had his Homestead at *Nafferton*. It is fascinating to conjecture why he was so called. Did he spend his nights prowling about the countryside and if so with what intent? Was he perhaps in cahoots with that equally mysterious Englishman Wealt (The Unsteady One) whose Homestead was at nearby *Welton*, and did they go drinking together? Certainly the two places are inextricably mixed by legend. Near Nafferton is the ruined tower of *Lonkin's Hall*, built by magic by Long Lonkin, the Wizard, for Lord Wearie of Welton, and never inhabited because, according to the ballad, 'payment got he never none'.

It was in the absence of Lord Wearie and his wife that Long Lonkin conspired with Orange, the nurse, to murder their child. She at least received her comeuppance:

> *Oh bonny sang the mavis*
> *That sang ower the brake.*
> *But sairer grat[1] Orange*
> *When they tied her to the stake.*

A Mavis is our word for a Songthrush and it is to be supposed that the same bird lent its name to the farm called *Mavis* as to *The Throstle*, *Throstle Nest* and *Thrush Hall*.

Another place whose name means in Old English the Homestead of the Unsteady One, is *Thockrington*, though one is left wondering whether his unsteadiness was due to his being a cripple or to over indulgence in mead. Anyone who has read thus far may well have wondered why our ancestors so often named after themselves the places where they settled. The use of a nickname such as this, of course, provides the answer, for it is one of the facts of life that (as distinct from houses) places are named not by the occupants but by the neighbours. How often, even now, when enquiring the where-abouts of a farm, do we ask for Smith or Jones rather than for the name of the place? And how much more so the inhabitants of the United States whose farms are so often known just as 'The Jackson Place'?

One can hardly imagine the inhabitant of *Scrainwood* himself christening his farm the Shrew's, or Villain's Wood, anymore than one can picture people at a later date giving themselves the kind of surnames with which they have since been afflicted. Nicknames (for this, of course, is how it all started) like the Unsteady One or the Shrew may be compared with some actually used by their Northumbrian owners, and collected by Dr Charlton, such as John Unkutheman, Adam Tesemen, John Dulp-in-the-drit, Elyas Blessed-blood, William Titmouse, and (from another source) Davy Sclavergobe. No wonder that a man called Wiseman had changed his name from Seliman. It is surprising indeed that Adam Aydrucken had not changed his to Sobersides or something of the sort instead of retaining a name which reminds one irresistibly of that verse of a Jacobite song aimed at George I, that runs:

> *And up wi' Geordie, Kirn-milk Geordie,*
> *He has drucken the maltman's ale,*
> *But he'll be nicket ahint the wicket,*
> *And tugget ahint his grey mare's tail.*

But even these names pale into insignificance in comparison with surnames to be found until quite recently in other parts of England such as Doggetail, Rotenhering and, most endearing of all, Strokelady.

There are a number of places in Northumberland that commemorate nicknames which are worthy of attention even if they do not aspire to such heights as these. *Embleton* was in 1200 Emlesdune, the Hill where a man known as the Caterpillar lived and *Kirkwhelpington* describes the Homestead of the People of someone nicknamed the Puppy, (to which was added a Church). *Thirston* appears in 1257 as Thrasterston, the Homestead of the Thruster, and *Lesbury* is the Stronghold of a man known as the Leech or Doctor.

Also incorporated in some of our names are diminutives: *Willimoteswick* the ancestral home of the Ridleys, for instance, was the Farm belonging to Little Willy, a Norman French nickname with the same meaning as Guillemot. *Flodden*, the Flat Hill, is a comparatively modern name, the battle having actually been fought where *Branxton Stead* now stands, denoting the Homestead of Brannoc (or Little Brand). Perhaps it was lucky (for the English) that the battle was fought at all for not long previously the locals had gone on strike when the Scots made a reconnaissance in force; refusing to fight unless their wages for the previous year were paid at 'open war' rates.

Peacock House belonged to Pecoc, or Little Peter, and *Wilkwood* to Willoc (the Old English for Little Willy). *Cramlington* and *Longframlington* are the Homesteads where the People of Scandinavians known respectively as Little Cram and Little Fram farmed and *Fram Hill* was probably named after the latter village but many years after.

This saga of names inspired to varying degrees by Scandinavians would not be complete without mentioning *Ghyllheugh* which represents the Spur of the Hill that sticks out into the Ravine. Or *Trygill* which may be called after an equally Scandinavian Ravine where there were Trolls or Goblins but more probably good Old English troughs (Northumbrian 'trows') as at *The Trows* in Coquetdale (which is called after the Pools in the Rowhope Burn). *Trowupburn* was known in 1352 by the pleasing name of Trollop which by 1542 had become Trohope, the Blind Valley frequented by Goblins.

The Red Comyn who was murdered by Robert Bruce and there-fore unwittingly precipitated the war with Scotland that finally led up to Bannockburn, was the owner of the castle at *Tarset* which (echoing Trewhitt of which we have already heard) is the Fold among the Fir (or Pine) trees.

Finally there is that charming and indisputably Scandinavian name, *Dingbell Hill* near Whitfield. Although described in 1862 as Dinmond Hill there is no doubt that it was originally the Thingwell or Parliament Hill. Indeed it was still known as Ving Well as lately as 1386. What presumably happened was that some Scandinavian was reminded by the hill of a similar place in his native land such as is still known in Iceland as Thingwell. There is no suggestion that it was used as such.

NOTE

[1] wept.

CHAPTER 5

I T is fair to say that in Northumberland, if in no other county, the influence of any race other than our Old English (Anglian) forbears, is irrelevant. Celts of course there were, and some of them will have intermarried with their Roman conquerors. The Romanised Celts, in turn, were driven into the less accessible valleys by the Angles but some will have remained and intermarried once more. The Scandinavians, as we have seen, left few traces and even the Normans, yet to come, had less influence in the county than probably anywhere else in England.

The Northumbrians, like their Cumbrian neighbours, continued to provide a pretty indigestible appendage to the map of England right up to Hanoverian times. They were, of course, involved not only in the Rising of the North but in the Pilgrimage of Grace, and it is only a couple of hundred years or so since they were out again in the '45. The history of the Northumbrian countryside, then, is very much an English history. We use the Old English words, even pronouncing them in much the same way, and with comparatively few exceptions the names of our villages and farms are English, and nothing else, and this is true whether they originated before or after the Conquest.

It is all the more important, then, that we should imagine ourselves in the shoes of these particular ancestors of ours when they were confronted with the wilderness of forest, moor and swamp that was later to be known as Northumberland. Having cleared our little patch, what are we to call it in order to differentiate it from a thousand other clearings? For it should not be forgotten that this was a world where rivers, streams, and hills might rejoice in largely incomprehensible Celtic names but, apart from a few deserted Roman forts, little else would be identifiable. In fact we would have to start almost from scratch.

One method would be to name places after the vegetation, either natural or cultivated, to be found there. Beside the North Tyne, for instance, grew a clump of plants with red berries ripening to yellow, now known to us as Cloudberries or Mountain Blackberries, and still often referred to as Noops, so it is not surprising to find that the Floodable Land where such Berries grew is called *Knoppings-holme*.

Bilberries, Blaeberries or Blueberries, call them which you like, are a common sight on moorland and elsewhere: hence *Blubbery Mires*, the Blueberry Swamp. But the berry that must have been commonest of all, because it was often known only as 'beger' or Berry, was the Cranberry which gives its name to *Barmoor*, to *Beggar Bog* and of course to *Cranberry Brow*.

What, then, are we to make of *Crowberry Hall?* Undoubtedly there is such a berry for 'at Whittingham in a plantation called Blackcock on the wild moor grows the black Crowberry, an acid fruit eaten by the Moorfowl'. It is a little disappointing, then, to find that the place takes its name from The Copse where Crows built.

And what about Hips and Haws; should they not be commemorated equally in our place names? In point of fact not only does *Brierden* describe the Valley where Briars grow but *Hepple* denotes the low-lying land where Hips, or Dogroses, are to be found and *Hawden* the Valley where the Hawthorn blossoms.

A common wild plant is Sweet Gale or Bog Myrtle, which gives its name to *Galewood*; *Gatherwick* is the Farm where Gaiter, otherwise Wild Dogwood, grows and *Lemmington*, near Eglingham, the Homestead where Brooklime (a kind of speedwell) is to be found. Yet *Lemington-on-Tyne* was once called, after the Laman Water Mill nearby, Lemendon; perhaps the Town at the Clearings.

A 'mor' can be wet or dry, so *Billsmoor* is the Swamp where such 'bilders' as Water Cress and Cow Parsnip are to be found. It is also possible that *Low Hocket* (once Hock Wood) has something to do with Hocks, or Mallows, in which case *Hocketwell* nearby would be the Stream where Mallows—those relations of the Hollyhock—grow. Two names that one might think were similarly derived are *Lear-*

mouth and *Learchild* but, although the first marks the Mouth of the Stream where Irises grow, the latter has nothing to do with Irises or, for the matter of that, any other wild flower, but describes the Slope where Leofric lived.

One would not think that Clover was sufficiently conspicuous to warrant naming a place after it. Nevertheless *Clarewood* was once Clavewurth, the Enclosure where Clover grew, and *Highclear* probably the place where Clover grew high up the hill.

Yarrow or Yarrow grass appears in *Yarridge*, which in 1479 was known as Yarow ryge, and in *Yarrow*, while *Yearning Hall* takes its name from the Hill (not Hall) where the Yearnin grass, used for curdling milk to make cheese, was picked.

Another grass to find its way into place names is Bent, a term which was applied not only to the grass of that particular rough and ready species but to any kind of sandy grassland such as dunes or, as in the ballad of Chevy Chase, to grassland in general. *Bent Hall* in North Tynedale and *Benks Hall* near Haltwhistle are two examples of this, while Rough Grass has also provided a name for *Finney Hill*. The names *Pry House* and *Pry Hill*, moreover, refer to the New Growth of the rushy grass known as Spart.

A word which is still used today to denote grass that has been allowed to grow for use during the winter is Foggage. *Foggeridge* was such a Ridge and *Foggett* such a Pasture.

Near *Beadnell*, that is to say the Low Ground by the sea where Bedewine settled, lies another *Bent Hall*, familiarly known as The Benty, a name that recalls the kind of affectionate diminutive that is comparatively common throughout the county. *Pinch-me-near*, for instance, now Fallodon West Farm (which should really be spelt Pinch-me-ne'er, implying a kind of prayer that the occupier should not be stinted of a living) is still often known as Pinchy.

Beggar-my-neighbour, now Craster West Farm, had the meaning of Outdo-my-neighbour and was invariably known as Beggary, while that strange name *Roguery*, near Whalton seems fairly pointless unless explained in somewhat the same way.

Most intriguing of all such names is *Peepy* which might have defied explanation were it not for Armstrong's map of 1769 in which a farm appears nestling among the trees on the north bank of the

Tyne, entitled Peep-I-see-thee.

So much for grass and its various associations. There is also a farm
in North Tynedale called *Rushend* which, for want of a better explanation, presumably started life at the End of a patch of Rushes.
Nettle Hill, can also in all probability be taken literally. When it
comes to *Thistlehaugh* and *Thistle Riggs,* however, the explanation
is not so straightforward as might at first seem likely. The real meaning would seem to be the Low Ground and The Ridge(s) respectively
that are Overshadowed by Higher ground; in the latter place the
old British Fort on the hill above.

Two other plants must be mentioned before we pass to the Heather,
Gorse and Bracken that have inspired the names of so many places.
Juniper in Hexhamshire used, not surprisingly, to be known as
Ginifer, the old rendering of the word which explains why Gin is so
called. The other plant is Watercress which, with The Spring at the
east end of the village, gave its name to *Cresswell.* The Pastures by
such a Spring became *Karswelleas* and the Row of houses *Kiersley-
well Row.* By the same token *Kersey Cleugh* and *Kershope* were the
Ravine and the Blind Valley, respectively, where Watercress grew.

It might be imagined that all those names beginning with 'Heath'
or 'Heth' were associated with Heather, but this is not in fact the
case. Yet *Heathery Shank,* now built on, was the Heathery Limb of
a Hill. *Heathery Tops,* known in the old days as Hungry House, can
be taken literally, while *Heathery Burn Steel* marks the Steep and
Heathery Ascent from the Stream and *Heatherwick* is the Farm with
Heather on it.

On the other hand *Heatherlea* is the Clearing of a man called Haethere and, just to make confusion worse confounded, out of three
places, at least, called *Heatherslaw,* one near Stamfordham (and more
often spelt *Hetherslaw*) is the Hill settled by another Haethere; the
farm near Edlingham is the Hill frequented by Harts, that is to say
Stags, and a third near Ford, quite possibly the same. There is,
however, a school of thought which connects the last of the three as
well as *Hethpool* with the goddess Hertha. It is more than likely,
however, that the latter is just the Heathery Pool.

Hetherington, once known as 'a village of considerable size' is the
Homestead founded by the People who lived on the Heath and

Hedley-on-the-Hill the Heather Clearing; *Black Hedley* being differentiated only by its Darker appearance.

It was at Hedley-on-the-Hill that the villagers used to be plagued by a kind of goblin known for some unexplained reason as the Hedley Kow. He had a nasty habit not only of disguising himself as a truss of straw or something of the sort, and then making off when one's back was turned, but of imitating people's voices so as to lure women out of the house. He would then take advantage of their absence to unravel their knitting, upset what was cooking or give the cream to the cat. In 1784 'it was commonly reported in the neighbourhood that a spirit called the Hedley Kow did haunt this place ... sometimes in the shape of a foal, sometimes of a man ... who waylaid unwary travellers and beat them senseless'. One suspects that some of these stories may be early instances of 'being kept late at the office'.

And so to Gorse which gives its name to *Whinney Hill*, and incidentally to *Winnows Hill*, which is a corruption of the same. It used to be said that 'no adder reaching the ground where Irish Cattle have lain can get away but dies', the evidence being that 'a dweller having a cattle gate on Winnoshill bought an Irish cow and fortunately for the owner no reptile would touch it'. The expression 'cattle gate' for a cattle pasture is worth remembering because the use of the word 'gate' in this sense appears in more than one place name, as will be seen later.

Whinnetley more probably denotes a Clearing that has Dwindled in size, presumably because of encroaching undergrowth, but *Prestwick Whins* without doubt describes the Gorse that grew near the Farm which provided the endowment of a Priest, if indeed it was not farmed by him. The Priest's Homestead, now *Preston*, and the Priest's Fen or Marsh, since known as *Pressen*, are examples of the same kind of endowment.

There are so many names into which the word Broom enters that only the less obvious ones need be mentioned such as *Broomley* the Clearing, *Broomhowe* the Hill and *Broomhope* the Blind Valley. *Brandon* also denotes a Gorse-covered Hill and *Branton* the Homestead where Gorse grows.

Bracken or Ferns, which are difficult to differentiate from each other in place names, are also in evidence in a number of instances. *Breckon Holme*, for example, is the Island or Flat ground by the river where Bracken grows. Not so *Breckney Hill*, or Heddon Laws as it used to be known. Five hundred feet high, it is the first hill of any size west of Newcastle and in consequence it has, throughout the centuries, been the chosen camping ground of Scottish armies attacking that city. In 1343 David Bruce pitched his camp there. Again in 1640, before the battle of Newburn, and in 1643, before besieging Newcastle, the Scots used the hill as a jumping-off place. Not unnaturally it bore a beacon on its summit and it seems probable that the real meaning is Beacony rather than Brackeny Hill.

Nor is *Farnham*, near Rothbury, related to Bracken or even to Ferns. It is, in fact, the old Thirnum, still known in 1542 as Tharnam, which between then and 1628 managed to change into Farneham (though in 1649 it appears again as Therneham). It signified the Homestead by the Thorns.

Yet *Farnley Gate* signifies the Road by the Ferny Clearing, *Farnley Grange* the Abbey Farm near the same, *Farneyside*, the Ferny Hill-side and *Farney Shield* the Summer Hut among the Ferns, or more probably the Bracken.

From wild plants to cultivated ones. The first thing to remember about the crops raised by our forbears is that they were grown by subsistence farmers, that is to say men who grew little more than was required for their own needs. The relative importance of their crops was therefore very different to what it is today; the principal object being to cultivate what was required for household use. A secondary consideration was the farm animals but these were not hand-fed to anything like the extent they are today. Cattle for instance were slaughtered and salted down whenever possible before winter set in or dragged through the winter on a diet of straw and a little hay, un-relieved, until the eighteenth century, at any rate, by turnips or anything much else; while pigs grouted for acorns and roots in the woods.

Beans and Peas, therefore, were of considerable importance for they formed a staple item of diet. Figures taken as recently as the seventeenth century show that they covered half the arable acreage of many counties, while on some farms no other crops were grown, for potatoes had only recently been introduced to this country and were never seen on a field scale until much later.

Although Defoe, travelling at the very beginning of the eighteenth century, found 'plenty of good bread and beer' along the coastal strip of Northumberland and in the valley of the South Tyne, the bread to be found in most of the cottages of the county would still have been made from pretty well anything that came handy and only in rare cases from Wheat. Beans, Peas, Oats, Barley and Rye all found their way into it when the occasion arose, Barley being the most popular because it was more filling!

Small wonder then that we find names like *Benridge*, the Ridge, and *Beanley*, the Clearing, where Beans were grown, while Peas were probably more important still, in medieval times and earlier; being either buttered or eaten as pease pudding. Yet (by an Irishism) none of the three names which would appear to be most obviously connected with them have probably any association at all. *Peafold* is more likely to be named after Peohtla's Cattle Fold while *Peasmeadows* and *Peasmead* may very well signify Meadows where Vetches, rather than Peas, grew in profusion.

There remains, however, that curious group of names, The Paise, The Pace Gate and Pace Bush. The only meaning that could apparently unite all these places would seem at first sight to have something to do with Easter. Pays, Pase and Pace were all, indeed, Pascal names, being derived from the Old English 'pasche'. Hence, also, the Paste Eggs which children used to be seen 'boolin' and jaapin'' on Easter Day. The difficulty, of course, is to understand why farms should have any connection with this particular season: even the provision of Easter dues to the priest would be difficult to connect with them.

It has been ingeniously suggested that as Greenridge, next door to The Paise, used to be known as Easter (as distinct from Wester) Greenridge, there was some kind of relation. An even less likely explanation arises from the presence of the Lead Road (of which we shall be hearing more later) not very far away, for it used to be the custom to pay the miners forty shillings a month on account and the remainder at an annual Pays.

Despite the presence of the plantation which rejoices in the name

of *Foulhoggers* (Muddy Swamp) some of the land may well have
been good enough to grow Peas and old records constantly refer to
the Paisland, the Peseland and even the Peseflat. It is fair to assume,
therefore, that *The Paise*, at any rate, owes its name to the Land
where Peas were grown. In fact the name of 'Thomas Armstrong of
the Pease' is to be found on the list of Roman Catholics compiled at
the time of the '45.

The Pace Gate and *Pace Bush*, however, present an altogether more
difficult problem when one considers the number of different con-
texts in which the word Pace is to be found, such as the Pace Hills of
Crookham and Buckton, the Pace Rock off Seahouses and the Pace
Bank in the Tyne.

Oats seem to have inspired only one name in the county and that,
rather unexpectedly, is *Overacres*. This incorporates the word 'haver',
our ancestors' name for Oats, while an 'aecer' is the Old English
word for the amount of land that could normally be ploughed in a
day, so that Acres came to mean Tilled Land and a farmer was once
known as an Aecer-mann. It might be conjectured that *Hiveacres*,
near Berwick, had the same meaning. Pronunciation, however, has
not greatly varied through the centuries, even if spelling has, and
the most likely explanation is provided by a nearby 'hythe' or Land-
ing Place—but where?

Nor, curiously enough, have *Overgrass* or *Overthwarts* a like meaning. Unless the communal or 'town' fields in which a proportion of
farming in Northumberland was carried out were strictly rectangular,
some of the tillage strips would inevitably be wedge-shaped. These
oddly shaped strips were known as Gores and it was these, and not
grass that gave their name to the farm that stands Above, or Over,
the Swarland Burn and is therefore known as Overgrass. Overthwarts
lies in the same kind of situation but some Scandinavian influence
has crept in which has resulted in the use of the word 'thwaite' for
an Enclosure.

Although a great number of little patches of oats must have been
grown on poorer ground and used to make 'crowdy' (the basic porridge of the North) the biggest cereal acreage will always have been
in 'bere', that is to say Barley,[2] which was used for making bread and
brewing ale. *Barhaugh* meant the low-lying ground where Barley was

grown and *Bearl* was originally Bere-hill. *Barley Hill* is one of those names which contain the same meaning twice. Originally it was Bere-law and therefore already meant what it does today.

Berwick-upon-Tweed and *Berwick Hill* owe their name to the manorial system (of which more later) for a 'bere-wic' in the North, like a 'bere-tun' (or Barton) further South, was the specialist Barley Farm of the manor (though *Barton* near Eglingham describes a Bare Homestead).

Ryal and *Great Ryle* are both Hills where Rye used to be grown. Then there is, or rather was, for the farm has since lost its identity, that delightfully named place *Redeford Pornleazes* which straddled the North Road just south of Belford. It must have been originally The Clearing(s) beside the Ford with the Soft or Yielding bottom, where Leeks were grown. It seems quite possible that these particular leeks were produced for the Monks of Holy Island, for Kale (the 'thin broth of the borders') played a major part in their diet. There appears, for instance, in their expenses of 1346 'three pounds of leek seed and one of onion seed 20d'. Indeed a local sympathiser, who could not bear to think of the reverend gentlemen having to live on such meagre fare, actually lent (but not gave) them a sum of money to expend on 'solidities'.

Beans are rarely to be seen in Northumberland nowadays and Peas hardly ever, for there are other parts of England better suited to their cultivation. Another crop that is no longer worth growing in the county is Flax but, in days when no textiles other than woollens and linen were available to the great mass of the population, it was absolutely essential to produce one's own raw material. Hence the fields of 'Lint' which were a common sight in Northumberland as elsewhere.

There used indeed to be a tradition that the linnet was called after the plant that produces flax (and, incidentally, linseed).

> *The Linty and the Lintwhite,*
> *The Laverock and the Lark,*
> *The Gooldy and the Goldspink,*
> *How many bords is that?*

Anyway the crop has left its mark on our place names. *Linacres* was one place where Flax was grown and *Lynup Hill* probably refers to a Blind Valley used for the same purpose. *Linton* on the other hand was originally the Homestead on the River Lyne, itself one of the Celtic words for something that Flows.

Lynehaugh, however, is definitely the Low Ground used for growing Flax while *The Linthaugh* is an amalgamation of four small farms originally known as the First, Second, Third and Fourth Lint Haughs where the crop was grown (once again) on behalf of the Monks of Holy Island.

It is noticeable that all the farms mentioned in this connection have something in common; namely a burn or river where the Flax was retted, or left to steep. Anyone who has lived in an area such as the Plain of Naples, and been subjected to that all-pervading smell so reminiscent of stale water from a flower vase, will sympathise with those who occupied neighbouring farms. Small wonder, also, that because in 1610, 'Ellinora Hidmers, Isabel Jefferson and Barbara Howey of Ponteland, Spinsters at Ponteland watered hemp in a river called the Ponte in which beasts were wont to drink ... they are to forfeit twenty shillings to the King'. The fibre may have differed, but not the nature of the offence which, incidentally, highlights the derivation of the word 'spinster' as the female of 'spinner'. When 'Alicia Pryngle, alias Whippy Towdy, spinster', was charged at Newcastle Assizes a few years before with stealing eighteen yards of cloth, she must probably have been similarly employed.

NOTE

[2] This term included both four and six-row varieties. The four-row variety was known specifically as 'bigg', hence the Bigg Market in Newcastle.

CHAPTER 6

'A FRUITFUL country, inhabited with pasturing people, which dwell in the summer season upon mountaines, and in Winter they remoove into the valleyes.' What Anthony Jenkinson wrote about Persia in 1562 might almost have been written about Northumberland. Indeed as late as 1720 Cox in his 'Magna Britannia' wrote about the Wastes of Northumberland (see Spadeadam Waste just over the Cumbrian border) as follows, 'There are several places in this county so called, especially in the valleys of Readsdale and North Tindale and the mountainous Places to them adjoining. In them you may see, as it were, the ancient Nomades, a martial sort of People, that from April to August lie in little Huttes (which they call Sheals, or Shealings) here and there dispersed among their Flocks'. He might well have added that these 'huttes' were normally circular and made of timber and turf: also that the Old English 'schele', later known as a Shieling, Shiel or Shield corresponds in nature (if not in the precise use to which it was put) to the Norse 'skali' to be found on the other side of the Pennines in such words as Portinscale—the Harlot's Hut.

Seeing that this kind of annual migration was normal to the county for hundreds of years it will come as no surprise to find a great number of names in which the word Shiel or Shield appears.

Low Shield, High Shield and, of course, *North Shields* just describe the situation of the shieling while *Shiel Hall* is the place where the original hut has been replaced by a Stonebuilt House, and *Bower Shiel* where there was a Cottage rather than a hut. A Plain or Open Expanse, rather than a hill-top, accounts for *Painshields* (near Felton) and *Panshields* near Whittonstall while *Craigshield* is named after its Crag.

Carrshield, a village which boasts, or at any rate used to boast, the highest school in England, was known in 1292 as Carrisideschield, meaning the Summer Hut on a Rocky Slope. *Halton Shields* takes its name from Halton, the Look-out Hill, *Sipton Shield* in Allendale, from the Sheep Stone (whatever that may have been) and *Woodley Shield* from the Glade in a Wood.

Other shielings were named after what went on there. *Hammer-shields*, for instance, where there was a Hammer Smithy that, like (the) *Smith's Shield*, may possibly have been occupied all the year round, and *Spital Shields* where there must have been a Shelter for travellers, as at *Coldharbour*. Within living memory there was a colony of huts in a wood at Throckley which was used as an Isolation Hospital (and now, though the old huts have been replaced, as a nudist colony). Nevertheless the word Spital has not invariably repre-sented a hospital in the modern sense so much as a Guest House where shelter, medical attention, or even education, might be given.

Oldmanshield, in North Tynedale is really a corruption of Alder-shiels, the Summer Huts by the Alders. There used also to be an Alderscheles in Coquetdale, the explanation of which is very dif-ferent. It happened to belong to the owners of Whittington and Aydon Castle; and was therefore known as Aydon Shiels of which the subsequent name was a corruption. *Aydon* (near Corbridge) in turn derives its name from a Meadow where Hay was made, just as *Aydon* near Alnwick denotes a Hill used for the same purpose. Yet there still exists in Hexhamshire an *Aydon Shiels* which, just to make matters more confusing, is named after Ealdwine whose name-sake used to summer his stock at a place near Haltwhistle whose name has since been corrupted to *Old Shield*. It was not long, however, be-fore Alderscheles began to assume the name not of Aydon but of Whittington so that it subsequently appears as Whickingate and, in 1663, as 'Adon Shiels alias Quicking Court'. In the end it became *Quickening Cote*, the Cottage or Outbuilding of the Whittingtons.

In fact the majority of shielings are named after their original owner rather than after their surroundings or other associations. Thus Abba gave his name to *Abbshields*, Cocca to *Cocken Shield*, Gerard to *Gairshield*, Kepe to *Keepershield* and Ranulph (probably) to *Ralph Shield* and *Raffshiel*.

Even *Battleshiel* has a personal association: it belonged in fact to the family of de Bataille (whose name originated from the Battle of Hastings) and the same probably applies to *Bateyshield*, though not to *Battlebridge*. Another shieling is to be found, rather surprisingly, in *Bolisher*, which was once Bolyopshell—the Summer Hut in the Blind Valley where Bodeling lived.

Davy Shiel really deserves a paragraph to itself. In 1344 it appears as Daveschole and probably owes its name to one of the Anderson family in which David was a common name. It is mentioned again in an account of the Jedburgh Circuit of 1623 when 'Jone Hall callit Chief, in Newbigging (Berwickshire) and Lancie Hall there' were accused of stealing a mare belonging to Roger Hall 'in Davieschiell in Northumberland' and were duly 'clengit' (caught). In the Lay of the Redewater Minstrel the place is noted for its 'gowks' (cuckoos).

The Ogle family who, among other vast possessions in Northumberland, owned *Sewingshields*, knew it as the Castle of the Seven Shields but there is little doubt that the place really owes its name to one Sigewine.

Burntshieldhaugh is the Low Ground where stands a Burnt-out Hut and *Espershields*, not far away, has been authoratively explained as East Burnt Shield. Nevertheless the evidence of early documents points to the place having been named after its original owner, in this case perhaps Osbricht. The word Parson, originally meaning a Person set apart for service of a church, is at least as old as the fourteenth century so *Parson Shield*, in Allendale, may well have belonged to, or provided the endowment for, such a priest.

There are also two or three Hills which, on closer acquaintance, may turn out originally to have been Shiels. One such is *Agar's Hill*, once Eadgar's Shieling. *Amos Hill* furthermore may well have been Eymundr's, *Anton Hill* Anthony's and *Gibb's Hill* Gilbert's.

Finally there are *Merryshields*, near Slaley, and *Merryshiels* at Bavington, each of them on some boundary or other and each deriving its name from the Old English word 'maer' meaning just that. Yet *Merryknowe*, like *Mirlaw House* signifies the Merry, or Pleasant, Hill. It is even possible that they were places where Merry Night used to be celebrated with all the feasting, sword dancing and other Christmas festivities that went with it.

*   *   *

Before proceeding any further, it may be as well to define more exactly the word 'hop' or Hope which appears in so many Northumbrian place names. It has been described as 'a small enclosed valley, a smaller opening branching out from the main dale, a blind valley', and it is this last description of a 'blind valley' that will be used throughout this book.

For all practical purposes a Northumbrian Hope is a strip of better land in a valley that is probably narrower than a Dene, less precipitous than a Cleugh (or Ravine) and more sheltered and less liable to flooding than a Haugh (the flat ground by a stream). A Hope, therefore, was quite a desirable possession consisting, as it did, of more fertile soil than was available further up the hills, and so in 1315 we find John Comyn, who was killed at Bannockburn, leaving in his will 'a number of Hopes in Northumberland'.

It might be thought that farms known simply as *The Hope* (as In Allendale) implied some particular measure of optimism but this idea would be just as mistaken as in the case of those other Hopes of which we shall be hearing so much. Another farm known as *The Hope*, near Edlingham, was described in the thirteenth century more precisely as 'Le Hope next to the White Stone'. Even the pathetically named *Hope Alone*, keeping its solitary vigil on the 'wrong' side of the Roman Wall, probably derives its name from the Lonely Valley of a Stream since renamed the Hope Sike. This kind of 'back-naming' is indeed quite a feature of our geography, and sometimes rather a misleading one.

Wholehope was originally Holehope, the Deep (or Hollow) Valley and *Fulhope* the Muddy or Dirty Valley. The latter has often been known as Philip and a document of 1663 refers to two places so named; one known as 'Fair Philip alias Halaricksburn' (that is to say the Stream where Alaric lived) and the other 'Foul Philip' which, on reflection, seems to be rather piling on the agony.

Startup, near Ponteland, was already in existence in 1737 but it is of course still possible that it is one of those fancy names describing the hopes, if any, of the first occupier. It is even more likely, however, because of its position, that the name signifies the Promontory that Sticks out into the Valley, and it may well be very much older than it appears.

Sweethope is the Valley where the pasture is Sweet; *Sinderhope* is the Southern Valley and the romantically named *Cairnglastenhope* commemorates a Heap of Glass-like Stones, perhaps of the same kind as Hodgson alluded to elsewhere when he wrote 'the sand beds of the Coquet have been celebrated for their beautiful pebble crystal'.

Then there are two or three places which one might not at first expect to be connected with Hopes at all. *Snope*, in Knarsdale, for instance, was originally Swanhope, a name sufficiently misleading in itself, for it meant the Snowy Valley. *Hoppen* just means At the Valleys and *Hopside* (most probably) the Valley Slope and *Wideopen* the Wide Valley.

For every Hope thus described, however, there are probably two or three whose names incorporate those of the original settler such as Cotta (or Coten) at *Cottonshope*, Blenkin (which is incidentally a Celtic name meaning the Man who lives on the Hill) at *Blenkinsopp* and a Miller at *Millershope*.

Robert Umfraville ('Robert cum barba', of whom we shall hear more) who later became Earl of Angus, retained among other lands in Northumberland, Suleshop, that is to say Syla's Valley and now known as *The Sills*. This estate was still being farmed on the 'open-field' system as lately as 1850 when Richardson was possessed of 36, Cresswell Baker of 28 and the 'three lairds' 16 pennyworths. A penny-worth seems to have corresponded, in this case at least, to about an acre and a half and the Lairds in question were Oliver, Coward and Hedley. Next door is *Silloans*, named after the Loan, Loaning or Lonnen that joins the Sills to the old Roman Dere Street nearby. It used once to be known as Blackburn.

Near Elsdon is *Headshope*, a place whose name was often corrupted to Egypt but which really denotes the Valley where a man called Head lived, while *Mohope Head*, known in 1510 as Upper Mollup, is at the Head of the Valley that was farmed by Mul (meaning perhaps the Half-breed).

With *Carshope* we meet a particular variety of names which describe the condition rather than the name of the settler, for this was a Valley farmed by a Churl, in other words, someone who had been freed from all obligations to his Lord. Other such names are *Charlton*, the Homestead and *Carlcroft* the Croft of the Churl or Freed

Villein, the Croft being the small piece of arable land farmed near his dwelling. An earlier name for Carlcroft was Stokershaugh, the Low Ground belonging to Styrkolr, or some such Scandinavian.

Another name of the same kind may be *Frankham*, the Village of the Franklyn, also a Free Man, though in a different category and not to be confused with such as the Freemen of Alnwick who have given their name to *Freemen's Hill*. Here was a pond formed by damming up the Freemen's Well, or stream. To quote the words inscribed on Armstrong's Map of 1769, 'Every freeman of Alnwick at his admissions is obliged to wade thro' the pond, which ceremony is said to have been ordered by King John'.

CHAPTER 7

I T is no accident that the three greatest battles ever fought on Northumbrian soil—Flodden, Homildon Hill and Halidon Hill —are named after Hills. Quite apart from the normal method of fighting a medieval battle by taking up position on a hill and then waiting for someone to be foolish enough to attack you, it was inevitable in such a hilly county that a great many place names should have been inspired by such obvious landmarks. Indeed our ancestors, presumably because the natural features of the landscape were more in their thoughts than is the case with their descendants, used a great number of names to describe an eminence according to its shape and surface. Nowadays we talk of a slope, a hill or a mountain and we have no time for the finer gradations which used to appear so important.

It so happens that the names of all three battles incorporate the Old English 'dun'. Flodden has been explained elsewhere. Homildon Hill was fought in September 1402 at what is now known as *Humbleton*. Earl Douglas, returning from Newcastle after a successful raid into Northumberland was overtaken and defeated there by Harry Hotspur, son and heir of the Earl of Northumberland.

At that time the place was known as Hameldun—the Cleft Hill— to which the word Hill has been added, as in so many other cases, out of ignorance. The same Old English word that denotes in this instance 'cleft' means in general 'mutilated' and from it also came the name for that essential adjunct to a threshing machine, the Hummler that knocked the awns off the barley—in other words, mutilated it. It appears again in *Humbleheugh*, the Cleft Spur of the Hill.

Fought in 1333, the battle of *Halidon Hill*, the third of the three, had been lost by an earlier Douglas who had also advanced—in this case to meet the army of Edward III—but with even less success. The original name of the place was in all probability Halig-dun—the Holy Hill—so that once again it was quite unnecessary to add the word Hill to 'dun' which, as must be pretty apparent by now, was a very common word for any kind of Mountain or Hill and, in special cases, for a Hill Pasture.

In the South of England 'dun' has in many cases become Down but this has been rare in Northumberland, a striking exception to the rule being *Downham* which just means At the Hills.

The Old English 'hlaw' was another favourite word in the county, denoting a Mountain, a Hill, or in some cases just a mound, so that a name like *Billy Law* very probably describes the Burial Mound of Billing, a settler whose namesake gave his name to *Billy Mill*.

In this context the word has much the same meaning as 'byrgen', a Tumulus or Burial mound, which subsequently became 'borran' or 'barrow' and was incorporated in a number of our place names. In Upper Coquetdale, for instance, there lie, some distance apart, *Barrow* and *Barrowburn*, both of which have been associated with the 'funeral mounds of the Ottadini', that Celtic tribe which gave the Roman invaders such a run for their money. Barrowburn itself seems to have rejoiced in the thirteenth century in a number of different names, among them Alribarns (which reminds one of the mysterious Alaric who lived at Carlcroft and who may also have farmed where these Borrans were) and Hepden (perhaps the Valley where Dog roses were to be found).

Such a Barrow on a Ness or Headland gave *Byrness* its name, while *Hebburn* and *Hebron* were High Borrans and *Bardon Mill* and *Birney Hill* the Hills marked by such Burial Mounds.

This is also the explanation (presumably) of *Carvoran*, which at first glance appears to be a Celtic name beginning with the usual 'caer' meaning a stronghold. The place used, however, to be known as Carboran and this spelling provides the necessary clue to the real meaning—the Burial Mound among the Rocks.

Hepburn Bell introduces, in addition, a Middle English word for a hill which appears again not only in Yeavering Bell but in other names which will be dealt with later.

The Laws and *Great Law* must by now be self-explanatory but *Shortlaw* has no connection with length, but with the Rock that Projects from the Hill in question.

There are Hills that were noted for being Dewy or Wet, such as *Dews Hill* (or the Dairy House Farm as it was sometimes called) and *Dues Hill*. And was it not at *Dewley* (Dewi-Law) that George Stephenson, the father of the railways, was given his first job by the Widow Ainslie? He earned twopence a day for herding her cows on the colliery wagon-way and shutting the farm gates at night. It was not very much but, after all, he was only eight!

If a Northumbrian were brought blindfold to the country above Bardon Mill, and the bandage removed, he could hardly help knowing what county he was in even if he could not see the Wall. The reason lies in the 'scarps' that lie to the north of the Military Road; a geological formation which results in the ground sloping fairly gently up and then dropping sheer so that a series of scarps looks something like the teeth of a giant's saw. A Height of this nature, which ends abruptly, or any kind of Projecting Ridge, Spur or Heel of Land, tends to be called a Heugh (from the Old English 'hoh', or Heel) and must on no account be confused with a Haugh, of which more will be heard later.

A Heugh would be easily quarried, so that it may not have been entirely due to the natural formation that *Brokenheugh* was so named. This is also the explanation of *Westerheugh* which is a corruption of Whetstone Heugh, just as *Westerhope* is the Blind Valley where Whetstones were quarried.

Or the Heugh might be named after something man-made, like *Penpeugh* where there was probably a Sheep-fold, as in the case of the Enclosure at *Pen's Close*. Or it might be named after the man himself, such as Hrobert at *Robsheugh* or Brynca at *Brinkheugh* (and, incidentally, at *Brinkburn*).

Not all 'hohs' have become Heughs, however, as witness *Sandhoe*, the Sandy Spur and *Ingoe*, the Spur covered with Pasture, while *Cambo* is a combination of two 'hill-words'. What has been described as an 'elongated ridge of drift and gravel' (or just a crest in general) is known in Northumberland as a Kaim, Comb or Cam. Cambo is such a Ridge that ends Abruptly.

Another very common ending to Northumbrian names is Side. *Helm on the Hill*, for instance, used to be known as Helmside. Now 'helm', as in the case of a helmet, means something pointed and so, in special cases, a Cattle Shelter (with presumably a pointed roof) and here we have the Cattle Shelter on the Hill or Hillside. On the other hand *Rimside*, where the Jacobites proposed in the rising of the '45 to give battle to General Wade and which is immortalised instead by the poem entitled 'The Black Sow of Rimside and the Monk of Holy Island', denotes the Pasture on the Rim (or edge of the Hill).

And so we come to such names as *Edge House*, just denoting a Ridge, and to *Edges Green*—a Grassy Ridge. The latter, however, used to have a more exciting name, being known as Slapy Stones from the Slippery Stepping-stones over the Pont Gallon burn. Yet *Edgewell* denotes, rather surprisingly, the Stream or Spring beside which Edge lived.

'Cnoll', the Old English word for a Hillock, became the Northumbrian Knowe, a word that has been applied often enough to lesser hills and moorland slopes but rarely to names of places. *Knowesgate*, however, describes a place where a Toll-gate stood among the Hills. *Loungesknow*, near Alwinton, was once known as Lounderingknow, which rather points to the place having been named after The People from the 'lund' or Grove.

Cliffs (usually in the sense of a steep slope) are to be met with in a few names; examples being *Cronkley* the Crooked Cliff, *Lonkley Head* the Top of the Long Cliff, and *Clifton* the Homestead by the Cliff.

Apart from such names as Mount Carmel, Mount Hooley and The Mountain Farm, the word Mount only seems to appear in one name and that is *Crammond Hill*, which describes, like *Bayldon*, the Crooked (in fact kidney-shaped) Mount.

Another word for a Hill which comes as something of a surprise is to be found in *Torlee House* near Kirknewton. Just south of the farm is the line of Celtic hill forts which crown such eminences as Yeavering Bell, Easter Tor and Newton Tors, the last two of which bear a common Celtic name explaining the meaning of Torlee—the Clearing on a Hill.

Having established some of the ways in which the different words describing a hill have been used to name villages and farms, it seems reasonable to look at a few of the variations on the main theme. Such, for instance, are the names derived from the Old English 'hlinc', meaning a Shelf. Thus *Linkey Law* describes a Hill with a Shelf or Plateau and *Link Hall* probably the same, with Hill being altered to Hall. *Lingley House* is also likely to have had a similar meaning (from 'hlinc-hlaw') while *Lynchwood* is the Wood on such a Plateau. The same word ('hlinc'), however, was subsequently used to describe any ridge, bank or sand-dune and so we get *Hadstone Link House*, named after the Links near Haddi's Homestead.

Then there are, of course, a number of hills 'with knobs on'. One of these is *Clinch*, near Ingram, which derives its name from 'Klinter' a word of Scandinavian extraction, meaning a Rock projecting from a Bank. A Hump is the general meaning of any Clench or Clunch in the county and in this particular case the name may have been inspired by the remains of the Bronze Age settlement nearby. *Knab Hill*, near Ancroft, probably means the same, though the derivation is different, while the Middle English 'knar' for a Rugged Rock gave *Knarsdale* its name.

Kip Hill takes its title from the ancient barrow that crowned it and from which a number of funeral urns were dug up. This barrow was known as The Chip, meaning Keep or Fortification, in the same way as Campfield, with its Celtic remains already referred to, was once known as Kippie Hill. *Kip Law* presumably derives its name from some similar Fortification. Another description is to be found in *Springhill* which has nothing to do with a spring (which in any case our forefathers called a 'well') but was surmounted by a Spinney. *Throphill* may have taken its name from a Crossroads nearby or even from the Neck of land on which it stands, but *Thropton* probably denotes the Homestead that was an Offshoot of Old Rothbury.

Then, of course, there are the Hills that are known by the name of someone who lived there, like Ceatta at *Chathill*, whose namesake's Homestead was at *Chatton*, or by their colour as in the case of *Grindon*—the Green Hill—and *Greenridge*. *Greenlawalls* denotes another Green Hill where the Foundations of an earlier building stood, and *Greenhead* the Watershed (in this case between the Tipalt and the Irthing) which was particularly Green.

Lightside describes a Hillside not so much light in colour as Lightly covered. This is also the explanation for the various *Greenleightons* which are Hills that are Lightly covered with Green (rather than White) grass. The farm near Rothley was known in the thirteenth century as Lytedun and the fact that there was a Light or Beacon on the Hill does not alter the fact that it owed its name to being sparsely covered.[3] The same must have been true, but in rather a different sense, of *Clennell*, the Hill that was Clean, or Free from Undergrowth, while *Wealside* was just the opposite, in other words a Wild, or Uncultivated, Hillside. *Greyside* was so called presumably on account of the Grey, benty nature of its grass or perhaps because of outcrops of rock.

A Hill might be called White for one of two reasons. The first and most obvious would be, as now, to differentiate hill land that was White in the sense of Whiteish Grass, from Black hill, so called because it was covered by Heather. The second, but no less valid, reason would be to describe a Wide Dry Expanse. A good example of the first is *Whitelee* (originally White Law) which has the honour of being the first farm in England—or, of course, the last if you happen to be climbing up to the Carter Bar from the South.

Whitley Castle has the same derivation with the addition of the old 'ceaster' to mark a Roman Camp. *Whitley Chapel* takes its name from a Chapel (or rather, an Oratory) that existed in medieval times. Subsequently it became a ruin and at some time in the seventeenth century was rebuilt. It became customary for the Quakers to hold their meetings on the Chapel Hill and so many onlookers wished to attend, out of curiosity, that in 1695 the Chapel was enlarged.

White Chapel, however, has quite a different derivation for it owes its name either to a Whitewashed Chapel (or Oratory) or to one that was noticeable because it was built of stone. *Whitfield* is called after a White, or Dry, Expanse of *Whitley Bay* a similar Clearing while *Whitten* is the Whitewashed, or stone-built Homestead, which was perhaps the same thing in so far as it must have been difficult to whitewash the mud huts of the early settlers.

Whitridge would have been noticeable for its White Grass and so would *Wheatridge* and *Wheat Hill*. *Whittle* however is the Hill with an Expanse of Dry Land, like the latter part of *Hepple White-field.*

Finally another trap for the unwary. *Whittonstall* was known in 1150 as Quickstunstal—the Tunstall or Homestead with a Quickset hedge—and had nothing white about it in either sense of the word.

Where there are Hills there are also, in the natural order of things, Valleys, and in Northumberland they usually take the form either of a Hope, a Dene (from the Old English 'den') or a Cleugh, which signifies a Ravine and comes from the Middle English 'cloh'. Normally a Dene is incorporated in some such name as *Bowsden* (the Valley where Bolla lived) but it may also appear in other and more confusing disguises. *Togston,* or Tocg's Valley, for instance, has no more connection with the Homestead (or 'tun') which it resembles than has *Gofton,* which was Gof's Valley, though once known rather surprisingly as Bandenside, the Slope above the Valley where Beans are grown. So *Dipton* is really Deep-dene and *Debdon* was originally the same, being again no more related to any kind of 'dun' or hill, than Hlyda's Valley of *Lysdon,* or the Valley with a Stream at *Weldon Bridge* or, indeed, the Winding Valley of *Chirdon.*

> *Hae ye ivver been at Elsdon?*
> *The world's unfinished neuk;*
> *It stands amang the hungry hills*
> *An' wears a frozen look.*

Certainly *Elsdon* 'stands amang the hungry hills' but is itself named after a Valley, in this case inhabited by one Elli. The story goes that this gentleman was a 'Danish giant' who lived on the Mote Hill, from which eminence he set forth to terrorise and plunder the country round about. One would not want, of course, to raise any doubts about the authenticity of this story but it should in fairness be pointed out that the so-called Mote (or Meeting) Hill is really the remains of one of the many 'motte and bailey' castles of our old friend Robert Umfraville, the man with the beard.

A Cleugh, like any other feature of the landscape, might be described in any number of ways. *Goldscleugh* for instance was probably called after a man named Golda; *Cleughbrae* is the Bank of the Ravine; *Greenleycleugh* is the Ravine with a Grassy Clearing.

The use of Dale (from the Old English 'dael') is comparatively rare in Northumbrian place names, other than the major valleys, but *Dalton* is the Homestead in the Valley and *Dally Castle* was built where there was a Clearing in the Dale.

In the early days of the eighteenth century a statute was enforced which prohibited Catholics from possessing a horse of a value exceeding five pounds. As might be imagined, among people like the Northumbrians and in times not far removed from those when they acknowledged 'no other king but Percy', this rule was honoured mainly in the breach. At the time of the '45 it fell to Sir William Middleton of Belsay to impound all the best horses at Hesleyside, as a result of which the Leadbitter of the day who owned Warden hid his most valuable horse at *Homers Lane*, a farm known earlier as Hollemarse and later Holmerscrofte, but actually signifying a Stream in the Hollow.

Subsequently the horse was brought back to Warden, lifted up to the loft above the stable with ropes and left there, surrounded by trusses of hay and bottles of straw. The bailiffs from Hexham, however, watched the place so closely that the horse could not be watered. In the end they had to be decoyed round the back of the stable to investigate the noise the horse was making; whereupon the owner lowered him to the ground, jumped on his back and never drew rein until he attained the comparative safety of Nafferton.

This use of Hole for Hollow is comparatively widespread in the county and serves to explain such names as *The Hole* and *Hole House*. By the same token, *Howburn* is the Stream in a Hollow and *Howdens* and *Howden Dene* the Hollow or Deep Valley, while *Bowser's Hole* was a Hollow well known as a Watering Place.

Hold House, near Ponteland, used to be known as Houlhill which was probably a modernised form of Houl-dun, hence the spelling of Hold and the meaning of the Hollow in the Hill.

NOTE

[3] The field next to the farmhouse has always been known as The Green.

CHAPTER 8

AMONG those who were indicted at the Newcastle Assizes of 1629 was 'Cuthbert Milburne, alias Cuddy of the Leam, for the felonious stealing of one filley and a colt the goods of Robert Laidley of the Hallbarns'.

Originally there must have been a hamlet of Leam clustering round the Peel Tower, the remains of which still exist, but as early as 1618 there appear 'certain lands called the Overleame', the precursor of what is now *Highleam* which, with *Lowleam*, now straddle the Peel in question.

It was thought at one time that the word 'Leam' had some connection with a highway. There is, however, no connection. Nor is there any doubt that Leam like *Lyham*, not far from Wooler, originates in the plural of 'leah', a Clearing. In the singular it usually appears as Ley and forms part of a great number of Northumbrian place names, corresponding to the Dutch 'Loo' as in Waterloo. Originally it meant a Glade or Open place in a forest where Grass grew, and in names such as Leam and Lyham this is probably the correct translation. In the great majority of cases, however, a 'leah' is a man-made, rather than a natural, Clearing while, later still, it became a Lea or Ley signifying a piece of Grassland.

When Edward I was making his final journey in order to 'hammer the Scots' he spent his last night before reaching Burgh-on-Sands, where he died, at *Bradley Hall* near Haltwhistle—in other words the Broad Clearing. If it had been a Long one it would have been known as *Langley*, *Long Lea* or *Longlee*; if Large (or Mickle[4]) as *Mickley* and, if High, as *Healey*. One example of the latter is the place near Riding Mill that used to be known as Temple Healey when in the ownership of that most powerful of all military orders, the Knights

Templars, whose possessions were extensive but their three vows of poverty, chastity and obedience honoured mainly in the breach. Another example is the Shelter, or Outbuilding, in the Clearing—now known as *Healycote* (near Longframlington).

Rather surprisingly, a Clearing (or the cultivated land into which it evolved) might, if the ground were Yielding, earn the name of *Softley* or, if in a Bright, Sunny spot, *Gladly*. It was these latter names that inspired Ralph Carr, when reading a paper in 1861 to his fellow Antiquaries in the Newcastle Society, to a height of facetiousness mercifully unknown in the present century. His subject was the 'Corrupt orthography of local names' in which he dealt with the following classes:

> '*Adverbial vulgarities*—Ly for Ley in terminations—softly for softley, Gladly for Gladley etc.
>
> *Sartorial vulgarisms*—Coat for Cote in terminations—Coats yards for Cotesyards....
>
> *Prandial vulgarisms*—Cold Pig for Cold Pike, Thropple for Throple....
>
> *Post prandial vulgarisms*—Wallbottle for Wallbotle....
>
> *Sputatory vulgarities*—Spittle for spital....
>
> *Decanal vulgarisms*—Crawley Dean for Crawley Dene.
>
> *Mountebank vulgarisms*—Stoco for Stokoe (Stokehoe)'.

What the subtle distinction between a vulgarity and a vulgarism is in this, or any other connection, we shall never know.

Fotherley is named after a Sheepfolder who operated there (perhaps the same thing as a Shepherd; perhaps not) while *Shipley* is the Sheep Pasture. Curiously enough, the latter once belonged to Simon de Montfort who, even if he was not the father of the English Parliament, was at least its inspiration. The Men of Shipley, for some reason, had a Dwelling elsewhere at Shiplingbotl, hence *Shilbottle*.

Shelley is the Clearing on a Shelf of land (such as we have met before) and *Shellacres* much the same; yet *Shellbraes* which, was earlier known as Shellawe, denotes a Bank with a Shieling, or Summer Hut, on it: it is *Shidlaw* that means the Hill with a Shelf. *Shilford*, however, is named after the Shallow Ford in the Tyne and *Shillmoor* after the Boggy Ground where Scufel lived, while *Shildon* was originally known as Schilyngdon, showing that it was the Hill of Scylf's People.

Other Clearings are named after the settlers who carved them out; Cocc giving his name to *Coastley* (once Costley Hope) Dudda to *Dudley*, Brynca to *Brenkley*, Hroda to *Rothley* and Ceofa to *Cheveley*. *Ardley* is Earda's Clearing and *Ardley Stob* the Tree stump nearby.

Or the clearing might be named after some landmark such as a 'well' or Stream, at *Wooley*, or a Stream in a Tiny Valley at *Waskerley*.

It is sometimes very difficult indeed to discover whether such names as these are in fact Clearings ('leah') or Hills ('hlaw') or even Cliffs. Thus *Tyneley* was originally the Tind-Law or Hill shaped like a Tine (of a fork); *Sharpley* is probably the Steeply Sloping Hill; *Heckley* the High Cliff; *Heighley* the High Hill(s) and *Stickley* the Hill where Stikki lived. When in doubt there are, however, two tests that can be made. The first is to ask the oldest inhabitant to pronounce the name, in which case a place such as *Crawley* will sound like Crawla—the Hill where Crows build. The second is to look for a stream which, if there has been a Clearing there, will undoubtedly be forthcoming while in the case of a Hill it may be some distance away.

Since Heughs have been mentioned, something should also be said about Haughs, the Northumbrian form of the Old English 'healh' which, in other parts of England just denotes Enclosed Land but, in our case, the Flat land that lies by a River or in the bottom of a valley. A good example is *Emmethaugh* where the Whickhope burn meets the North Tyne so that it is the Haugh where the 'ea-mote', that is to say the Waters Meet, just as *Mote Hill* at Wark on Tyne and *Moat Law*, near Kirkheaton, describe the Hills where the people meet.

It was at Emmethaugh that the fate of the Wicked Lord de Soulis was sealed. This gentleman was noted throughout the Border as a most unpleasant character, and a sorcerer to boot. He lived at Hermitage Castle in Liddesdale which was afterwards to be the home of Bothwell, and the scene of Mary Queen of Scots' visit to him when he lay wounded there.

It was in the days of Robert Bruce, however, that there lived in

North Tynedale a man who rivalled de Soulis in his tremendous strength and who was known in consequence as the Cowt (Colt) of Kielder. One day the Cowt decided with his friends to hunt deer in Liddesdale, right under his rival's nose. Before doing so he took the wise precaution not only of riding three times widdershins (that is to say, against the sun) round the Kielder stone but of sticking a sprig of rowan in his helmet.

De Soulis, however, was equal to the occasion. He invited the Cowt to dinner, an invitation which, in the circumstances, he cheerfully accepted, and then ambushed him. In escaping over the burn which serves Hermitage almost like a moat, the Cowt's helmet fell into the water and with it the luck that he had sought, whereupon he was held under water till he drowned. His friends, however, determined to avenge him:

> *There be twenty lords in that border....*
> *They have set a meeting at Emmethaugh*
> *And upon the Lilienshaw,*
> *They will be wroken of Lord Soulis,*
> *His body to hang and draw.*

In point of fact the 'lords' were even better than their word for they succeeded in seizing their enemy and boiling him in a pot, and if proof is needed of this culinary extravaganza it is to be found in the immense cauldron that used to be preserved near Hawick.

A farm whose name is, rather surprisingly, derived in much the same way as Emmethaugh is *Edmond Hills* near Ancroft. The present name is a corruption of Hermit Hills which, in turn, was a corruption of Emotehill—the Hill where the Waters Meet. 'Ea', for Water, appears again in *Ewart*, the 'Worth' or Homestead by the Water, which is hardly surprising when one considers that the Till and Glen, between them, enclose the place on three sides. Similarily *High Ewart* is in a bend of the River Blyth. Yet *Ewartley Shank* would seem to have a totally different derivation. It probably denotes the Projecting Part of the Hill where there was a High Homestead.

There is, of course, another method of describing the meeting of waters, or the addition of a tributary to the main stream, and that is by alluding to it as a fork or, in Old English, a 'twisla', a word that also denoted the land within the fork. And so we get a name like *Haltwhistle*, which was known in 1240 as Hautwisel and provides an example of what appears to be an extreme rarity in Northumberland —a mixture of Old English and Norman French; the name describing the Junction of Streams by a Height, or Hill. The same word is also to be found in *Twizell*, and most probably in that delightful name *Whistlebare*, the Grove or Copse by such a Junction.

Yet another Old English word for a river-fork was 'twang', meaning Tongs, or anything of that shape, and this is the explanation of *Tongues* which lies between the Coal Burn and the Black Heddon Burn, and also of *Burntongues* in Allendale.

But, to return to Haughs, *Angryhaugh* is the Grazing Haugh, the same Old English word for a Pasture appearing in *Angerton*, the Grazing Farm, and in *Ingram* the Grassland Village.

Elyhaugh, near Edlingham, most probably derives its name from some Alders though it is possible that the place may be connected with the same Illa who gave his name to the Hill of *Elilaw* and whose namesake lived in the Wood of *Ellishaw* near Otterburn. This is the place, at one time graced by a leper hospital, that originated the expression 'he'll be left on the haughs anunder 'lishaw if he dissn't hurry on'; the point being that this is where the Rede deposits its burden after a flood.

The broad valley of the Tyne at *Widehaugh*—known in the Thirteenth century as Widehalg-in-Develstone (Dilston)—contains its own derivation and a similar valley (of the Tipalt burn this time) explains *Wydoncleughside*—the Steep Bank of the Broad Valley. Not far away are the Water Meadows of the wide valley at *Wydon Eals*, near which took place the event so graphically described by Robert Surtees in one of those bogus ballads of his that are better than the real thing.

> *Hoot awa', Lads, hoot awa'*
> *Ha' ye heard how the Ridleys and Thirlwalls and a'*
> *Ha' set upon Albany Featherstonehaugh*
> *And taken his life at the Deadmanshaw;*
> *There was Willimoteswick*
> *And Hard Riding Dick*
> *And Hughie of Hawdon and Will o' the Wa'*

I canno' tell a', I canno' tell a'
And mony a mair that the deil may knaw.

Some of these names we shall meet again: in the meanwhile it is
perhaps worth pausing for a moment to look at this word Eal, meaning literally an Island or piece of Floodable Land. *Winter Eale* then,
explains itself, as do *Eals Farm* and *Wide Eals* while *Eelwell* would
be named after the Spring rising in such land.

Another name that, however improbable it may seem at first sight,
may have a similar origin, is *Plankey Mill*. Plankey Ford, nearby, was
known in 1673 as 'Planky Ford alias Nakedale' while in 1537 a certain
Thomas Knagg had been sued in respect of Naked Ele (the Necked
Eal, which undoubtedly it is). Now Playford in Suffolk is known to
have been a Ford where Games were played. Could Plankey be the
Play-Necket or Neck of Floodable land where Games were held?

But, to return once again to our Haughs; *Greenhaugh* is self-explanatory; *Kirkhaugh* was named after a Church or Chapel and
Shothaugh after a Hut that stood there. The Stream beside which
yet another Scufel lived appears in *Shilburn Haugh*, and someone
called Moll probably gave his name to *Mouldshaugh*. Strange as it
may seem, *Filberthaugh* has nothing whatever to do with nuts but a
good deal to do with a man called Hildeburgh.

Fairhaugh, like *Fairmoor* and the Copse of *Fairshaw* is a Pleasant
place, and so is *Fairley* (previously Fairlaw and Fairhill) with its
appendage *Fairley May,* in other words the Farm on the Boundary
of Fairley. Yet *Fairplay* is the place where Deer Play.

And so to *Pauperhaugh*. From the pronunciation, one would expect this to be one of those places like *Piper's Close* for which the rent
used to be so many pounds of that rare commodity in medieval times,
Pepper. In 1100, however, it was spelt Papwirthhaugh, the Haugh
farmed by the man from the Homestead founded by a man called
Papa.

There are, of course, any number of Haughs which will be mentioned in due course: it only remains to deal with one other here
and that is *Snabdough*. In the fourteenth century it was known as
Snabothalgh—the Haugh with the Little Projecting Rock.

Finally there are a few 'healhs' in the county which, although the meaning is the same, have not become Haughs but Hales, or something similar. *Howtel* for instance is the Low Ground with a Holt or Wood while *Etal, Seghill* and *Tughall* represent Low Ground settled by Eata, Siga and Tugga respectively.

NOTE

[4] Mickle comes from the Old English 'micel', meaning Much; hence 'many a little makes a mickle'. In Scotland the word means Little and so, 'mony a mickle maks a muckle'.

CHAPTER 9

The Protestant glebe house by beech trees protected
Sits close to the gates of his Lordship's demesne.

WHEN John Betjeman wrote this, and rhymed the last word with 'plain', he was alluding to something that is still part of the geography of Northumberland even if we often pronounce it 'demean'. It was in fact, for all practical purposes, the Home Farm of the Lord of the Manor, consisting of the best of the pasture adjoining the Manor House as well as a number of strips in the arable fields that were common to all the villagers. *Colwell Demesne*, then represents (near enough) the Home Farm of the Manor where there was a Cool Spring.

Another form of the word which, in pronunciation, if nothing else, is probably a good deal nearer to the original, is Mains. *Mainsrigg*, for instance, is the Ridge of Whitfield Demesne, and *Mainsbank* was known in the fifteenth century as 'Lez mayns de Stamfordham', with much the same meaning. *West Mains* near Haggerston Castle, moreover, is nothing to do with a main coal seam, nor is it necessarily more important than its neighbours, but is once again part of the original Home Farm.

It may well be asked how and when a Lord of the Manor, or indeed the Manor itself, has suddenly appeared on a scene that has so far been very largely English. The reason, of course, is that although the Norman Conquest exerted no immediate influence on a part of the country as distant and recalcitrant as Northumberland, by 1068, at any rate, the Normans were really beginning to exert their authority in the county. Unfortunately the strenuous resistance put up by the northern earls resulted in the invaders adopting a scorched earth policy which left the county barren and backward for hundreds of years.

At the time of the Conquest the population of the whole of England probably did not exceed a million and a quarter, while in what we now know as Northumberland it is unlikely that there were more than twelve thousand inhabitants, so they cannot have been very thick on the ground. The countryside still consisted largely of forest out of which scattered clearings had been carved, some of which would be several miles wide, containing small hamlets known as often as not as towns, or at any rate 'tuns'. Other clearings were just big enough to contain one of those isolated farms that differentiated the North of England from the Midlands and South, where sizeable villages were the order of the day and single farms or hamlets the exception. Only the very best and easiest land was cultivated and in very few cases had anyone settled at over a thousand feet.

Although the Normans radically altered the face of the countryside by the fires that they lit and the slaughter that they caused, their effect on our place names was comparatively small. There are none of those euphonious names that one finds elsewhere, such as Coatham Mundeville, Sutton Courtenay or Stanstead Mountfitchet—with one exception, *Seaton Delaval*. Seaton, the Homestead by the Sea, has given its name to the *Seaton Burn* and to the village of that name but it is to the family that came over with the Conqueror from Laval that the other Seatons in the valley owe what fame they enjoy. Of *Seaton Lodge*, for instance, the third baronet boasted that it was 'the finest thatched house in the kingdom'. It was the Delavals, also, who created *Seaton Sluice* by building water-gates at the mouth of the burn, which dammed it up until the tide went out, when the gates were opened and the current scoured the harbour.

Probably the greatest difference that the Normans made to Northumberland was in the emphasis that they placed on the manorial system, in which the key figure was the Lord of the Manor, whose demesne in turn was thte focal point of the village over which he ruled. A typical manor house at this point of time probably varied little from that later described by Chaucer as consisting of two principal rooms, one (down) being the Hall and the other (up) the Bower or Women's Chamber, with a Bur or Buttery below.

This word Bower, signifying somewhere secluded or sheltered, we have already met both in Bower Shield and in Harlow Bower. Then there is *Cumberland Bower*, north of Berwick, which is more than usually difficult to explain. Until early in the eighteenth century it was known as Crawford's Meadows. In 1769 it was The Bower Farm and not until 1809 does it appear in its modern guise. Now 'Butcher' Cumberland is known to have passed that way on his journey from Felton to the fateful field of Culloden in 1746. Perhaps he sheltered there but the fact was not advertised until later, when tempers had had time to cool.

Roses Bower (of which there are two at least in the county) is another problem, for who, or what, was Rose? The farm in North Tynedale was a stronghold of the Charltons and had a Healing Well but Howard Pease 'could find no legend but thought there must have been a fair Rosamund who had been in love with the Chief of the foremost grayne'.[5] Near Matfen, and not far from the remains of a bridge that used to carry the Roman road known here as Cobbs Causeway, is another farm of the same name for which the explanation also seems to have been lost.

Roseden, which might be thought to provide a clue, signifies nothing more exciting than a Rushy Valley but *Rosebrough* provides a possible answer for it used to be known as Osberwick (Osburgh's Farm) so that Rose may not have been so feminine as she appears.

But to return to the Norman Manor. This consisted not only of the Manor House and Demesne but of the various dwellings of the villagers, each having his Toft and Croft, that is to say the plot of land containing his house and the small enclosure of meadow or arable land adjoining. This last was a kind of allotment over which the owner had complete control (unlike the strips he tilled in the Common or Town Field). Place names containing the word Toft are rare in the county and, where they do appear, generally signify a Deserted Site: thus *Toft Hill*, *Toft House* and *The Tofts*.

In addition there would be a Pinfold into which were driven any straying animals; the Lord's Fishpond, his Dovecot, his Warren and his Mill. A Fishpond was also known as a Stank and this, married to the Stream which fed it, gave *Standwell* near Harlow Hill its name, rather than the commanding position which might be thought to explain it.

The Dovecot was at least as important, and far more so than could reasonably be expected today, for when carcases, and particularly beef and pork, had to be salted down to keep over winter, fresh meat of any kind assumed a particular importance. Moryson, who travelled extensively on the continent in the reign of Elizabeth I, was convinced that 'no kingdom in the world hath so many dove houses'. He might have added that the number of pigeons eaten and sold from them was also enormous. In the case of one of the Cambridge Colleges alone, the figure in the fifteenth century amounted to two or three thousand a year.

There are at least two farms in the county known as The *Dovecot*. Where the steading of one of them now stands (near Hartley) there once flourished a dovecot belonging to Edward Hussey Delaval which in 1814 was broken into, and there was the devil to pay. Indeed in the early days of the nineteenth century, pigeon dung was still sufficiently plentiful to be classed as a major contribution to soil fertility. A name less obviously connected with pigeons is *Cullercoats* which was originally Culfre-Cots, meaning (literally) out-buildings devoted to Doves.

Next on the list is the Warren where the rabbits were, of course, strictly preserved for they also provided a valuable source of fresh meat for the Lord of the Manor. *Warreners House* near Morpeth marks the home of the official responsible for this preservation, and he probably had to be on his toes to prevent poaching. At the Newcastle Assizes of 1610, for instance, Lionell Strother, gentleman (sic) was charged with having broken into the free warren of Henry, Earl of Northumberland, and with stealing twenty rabbits worth ten shillings.

Efforts have been made to explain *Coneygarth* as having nothing to do with conies but to have originated as the King's Yard or Farm (as *Kenton* is the King's Homestead) on the basis that the name was derived from a Scandinavian word virtually identical with the German König. In 1531 Earl Percy is recorded as having presented his chaplain with 'one little grassground of myn called Conygarth' but this does not in any way alter the real meaning of the name, which

comes from a perfectly good Old English word 'coning-erth' meaning a Rabbit Warren.

The same Moryson who was so impressed by the number of
pigeon houses drew attention also to 'great plenty of conies, the flesh
whereof is fat.... The German conies are more like roasted cats than
the English conies'.

Mills, known to our forefathers as Milns, were of course a common
feature of the countryside. The whole process of bread-making seems
to have been fraught with restriction. No village woman baked her
own bread but had to take her flour to a communal bakehouse, traces
of which have survived (as at Dinnington) almost to the present day.
Milling the flour in the first place was a jealously guarded perquisite
of the Lord of the Manor. For instance, in a charter of 1328 granting
a mill to William de Burneton (that is to say *Brunton*, or the Homestead by the Ouse Burn), it was laid down that none of the farmers
'shall mill corn otherwise than at the said mill ... nor shall the
tenants have hand mills. If such be found, William's men may break
and remove them'. The normal practice was for the Lord's men to
visit the houses of the villagers periodically and to break the top, or
thinner, quern of any hand mill they found.

Mills, generally speaking were of three kinds. There were Flour
Mills driven by the wind such as that at *Mill Hill*, near Mason, which
belonged to the Monks of Newminster Abbey; Flour Mills driven
by water, and Fulling Mills. The Fulling Mills were worked by men
who tramped or 'walked' the cloth, and subsequently by heavy ham-
mers driven by water power, and were known as Wealc Milns. It is
not long since *Hesleyside Mill* was known as *Walk Mill* while there
is a farm beside the Wansbeck at Kirkwhelpington which still bears
that name. Another example, further down the Wansbeck and connected to it, according to the records of Newminster Abbey, by a
ditch is *Abbey Mill*.

Yet another was near *Warkworth*. It might be imagined that this
name might have some connection with the Walkers, or Fullers, who
worked there, but in fact it signifies the Worth, or Homestead, of
Wearca, the seventh-century Abbess of Tynemouth. Nowadays the
place is, of course, famous for its Hermitage and its Castle, which
provided the setting for several scenes of Shakespeare's Henry IV.

In 1538 its keep was described with unconscious humour as a 'marvellous proper dongeon'.

Another step in producing cloth is its final stretching, a process that must have given *Tenter House*, in North Tynedale, its name.

The stones for the corn mills had to come from somewhere and one of the sources must have been *Whirleyshaws* (or Quarry in the Copse) near Acklington. Another would be *Minsteracres* which, despite the presence nowadays of a community of Passionist Fathers, owes its name not to any connection with an Abbey but to the fact that it was christened Millstone-Acres. The Clearing where millstones (Querns) were quarried is now known as *Wharmley*, while it seems probable that *Nilstone Rigg* was once Mill-stone Rigg.

The actual number of Norman names in the county, as has already been pointed out, is not very great. *Haggerston*, referred to earlier in this chapter, signifies the Homestead of someone known to his Norman compatriots as Hagard, the Wild or Strange one, or at any rate of a man whose family name was thus derived. *Haggerston Flowers* is an attractive title which has nothing to do with flowers but is derived from a word meaning the Flat Ground at the Base of a Slope. *The Flothers*, near Slaley, however, takes its name from a Swamp, that is to say where water flows over, while *Flotterton* is the Homestead where the road passed over such a Swamp, possibly on some kind of pontoons.

Reference has been made to the Delavals, who were also connected with a Hill where Calves are grazed—that is to say Callerton. Originally there were three Calverdons. The first, now known as *Black Callerton*, from the outcrops of Coal nearby, was Calverdon Delavale. The second was Calverdon de Valence, called after the family who owned that part of the land now known as *High Callerton*. The third was Calverdon d'Arreyns and hence *Darras Hall*. At one time the land immediately south of the Pont was known as Callerton-by-the-Water.

This latter family, who hailed originally from Airaines, near Amiens, and were sometimes known as Arenis, may also have owned the farms near Whittonstall now known as *Airey Hill* and *Airey Holm*, the last-named taking its name from the Water Meadows of the neighbouring stream.

Plessey Checks denotes a place where Coal, coming from the nearby colliery, was checked, and is called after the family of de Plessis who, in turn, took their name from Plaissiet. The derivation of this French word is in itself worth looking at for it also explains *Plashetts*, a name that appears at Bavington and again in North Tynedale. It means land that has been enclosed by a Plashed or Plaited fence and therefore, probably, a Park.

Whiskershiels, near Elsdon, suggests the question 'when is a whisker not a whisker?' Like *Wishaw*, near at hand, it is named after a certain Wishart whose Summer Huts these were. Wishart, in turn is the anglicised form of the Norman Guiscard which, when translated, turns out to mean Wise Beard so the modern rendering is not so far out after all.

This kind of allusion to facial fuzz was not uncommon. The first Percy, who landed with the Conqueror, was known as Al Gernons (meaning 'with the Whiskers') and Algernon has been a family name of the Percies and their descendants ever since. Near Bingfield is a farm known in the reign of Edward I as Beaumont Hamlet; in that of Henry VIII as Beaumontfelds and nowadays as *Beaumont House*. It was presumably owned by a Norman family whose name was French for Beautiful Hill. This became yet another possession of the Umfraville family who supplied Northumberland with Robin Mend-the-Market. The latter earned his name from the fact that when supplies were short he could always be relied upon to rectify the situation at the expense of the Scots. The most famous member of the family, however, the afore-mentioned was Robert-with-the-Beard.

Bowmont Hill, on the other hand, is named after the Bowmont Water close by, which in turn used to be known as Bolbenda, a name which may have been inspired by the Bends that are such a feature of that river. This same notion of Bends might be thought for reasons which are real, if not apparent, to have inspired the name of *Bearsbridge* near Whitfield and also of *Bay Bridge*. In point of fact the former, like *Barrasford*, is called after the nearby Woods for which one of the Old English terms was 'bearwas', while the latter has either much the same derivation or else the name denotes the Bridge where the river is Banked up or obstructed; perhaps to form a dam.

Blanchland, nearby, owes its title to its Abbey which was founded by monks who were called (after Prémontres in Normandy) Premonstratensians. The Abbey was affiliated to that at Blanchelande, near Cherbourg, whose name in turn meant the White Glade or Lawn.

Pallinsburn may be the Stream where Paelloc's people lived: on the other hand it could have Norman associations and denote the Stream where there was a Pavilion, a word which has survived in Scotland as Pavilioun, a Summer Seat.

Then there is *Puncherton* which in 1086 was in the possession of Robert de Pontchardon, who was called after a place of the same name in Normandy that means Thistle Bridge. *Barneystead* and *Garretlee* were places where Bernard had his Farmstead and Gerard his Clearing, while another Norman called Scrimer or Escrimer (the Fencer) had his Homestead at *Scremerston*.

Sir Hugh Gubiun (or de Gobyon) was Sheriff of Northumberland from 1292 to 1296 and held the Manor of *Hepscott* (where Hebbi had his Sheep-shelter or some other kind of outbuilding). It is not surprising, therefore, to find *Gubeon* named after him or his family. *Fulcherside*, near Mickley, was the Seat of William de Feugers, another Frenchman, but as he came from Fougères in Britanny and the first that was heard of him was in 1780, he can hardly be described as a Norman.

Chertners takes its name from The Chartenay family and *Vauce* is a corruption of Vaux, later anglicised to Falkes, a family name which appears also in Vauxhall. *Guyzance*, likewise, is a corruption of Gysnes. Here lived a Norman of that name who dedicated to St Wilfred de Gysnes a chapel at nearby *Brainshaugh*, which takes its name from the Low Ground by the river where there was a Borran or Burial Mound.

Finally there are a few names, given to places by the Normans, that describe their situation. The use of their word 'prud' or Proud for something that stands out (like proud flesh) gives *Proud Hill*, near Hedley, its name and also *Prudhoe*, the Spur that Stands Out. *Beaufront*, in turn, is the Fine Brow and no one who has admired its position overlooking the Tyne would deny the aptness of the name.

Bellasis, with its wonderful old pack-horse bridge (whose predecessor was known to the monks of Newminster as the Bridge of Horton) is the Fine (or Beautiful) Seat of some Norman immigrant.

Bellister is another of the same sort, the name denoting in this case a Fine Site ('estre') but this is not to say that all Northumbrian names beginning with Bel are of Norman origin: far from it. *Bellion* and The *Belling* probably describe Hill Pastures and *Bellridge* the Ridge of a Hill. This use of the word Bell for a Hill also appears in *Bellingham,* the Village of the People who lived on the Hill. Yet *Belsay* describes the Spur of a Hill where Bill (that is to say, Little Bilheard) lived. *Belford*—if it is the same place as Bellanford, mentioned in a document of 843—would signify the Ford beside which a man called Bella settled.

Belshill, nearby, was once famed for its three-storey granary where grain was collected and stored before being exported from Warenmouth, the port of Bamburgh. In all probability the place was originally Bell-Shiel—the Summer Hut on the Hill. The Waren burn takes its name from the Celtic 'pharned', meaning an Alder stream; hence also *Warenford* and the Homestead of *Warenton. Warenmouth* itself was once important enough to rank among the hundred places in England to enjoy not only the title of Borough but, as a result, a royal charter allowing it to engage in trade and, within limits, to govern itself.

Alas, the port was silted up by the mud of Budle Bay and its place, though no longer as a port, was taken by *Newtown,* described in 1330 as the 'New town on the Warneth'.

The advent of the Normans, indeed, seems to have resulted in a number of New Settlements of one kind or another. The New Castle which gave Monkchester its modern name of *Newcastle upon Tyne* was begun before the end of the eleventh century and the New Abbey of *Newminster* in 1138. *Newton* near Stocksfield was a New Homestead some time before 1346 when it first appears in history, and *Newton Underwood,* which signifies a New Homestead that is In (and not below) a Wood, is probably older still.

Newsham was described in 1296 as At the New Houses and *Newham,* near Belsay was already the New Village in 1245. By the time *Newbrough* appeared on the scene, the word 'burh' had probably lost some of its signficance as a Fortified Place and assumed more of the meaning that it has today of a borough or town. Certainly it was known as Nieweburc as early as 1203, in contrast, presumably, to such places as *Lonborough* (the Long Fortification) *Burgham* (the village by the Stronghold) and *Burradon* where the Fortification surmounted a Hill.

Newlands Grange is interesting because it reminds us of the fact that the clearance of land for farming still went on apace under the Normans; the cleared soil being known as New Lands. It also introduces the word Grange which, coming into use with the manorial system that the Normans brought with them, springs from the Latin 'granum', a granary. It was in fact the 'off-farm' where grain was stored or rent paid in grain, so that in the North of England it came to mean any isolated farm, though more particularly one belonging to a monastery.

A very common name in Northumberland is *Newbiggin*, the first mention of which is that of Newbiggin-by-the-Sea in the twelfth century. Biggin is a Middle English word (that is to say, one brought into use between, roughly, 1100 and 1500) for a Building. A much more ancient name, and possibly the granddaddy of them all, is *Newburn* which was the New Burgh or Castle that took the place of the palace of the Northumbrian kings at Walbottle. It was in the church here that in 1072 Oswulf, who had been deprived by the Conqueror of his Earldom of Northumberland, smoked out his successor Copsi, and murdered him.

There remains one name which one would not readily associate with the Normans and that is *Delegate Hall* (or Delicate Hall as it has sometimes been known). The clue to its meaning is to be found in the fact that it appears in 1296 as Dewillawe, that is to say D'Eiville's Hill. In point of fact it is almost next door to *Dilston*, the Homestead of the D'Eivilles and near enough to the Devil's Water which also bears their name.

NOTE

[5] Weight is lent to this theory by Hodgson who writes that Robert Clifford, who fell at Bannockburn, 'had children by a favorite of the name of Julian, for whom he built a house in the park of Whinfell, called after her Julian's Bower'.

CHAPTER 10

APART from St Oswald, whom we have already encountered at Heavenfield, and St Aidan who founded the monastery on Holy Island, there are three saints who have been particularly associated with Northumberland: Cuthbert, Ninian and Brandon.

The first of these, and without any doubt the best known, is thought to have spent his boyhood at *Wrangham* which was then known as Hrangaham. It seems probable that the meaning of the name was not the Wrang, or Crooked, Village as was once thought, but the Village of the People who lived by the Fallen Tree.

St Ninian's name was always associated with Whittingham Fair, which used to be known for some inexplicable reason as Trunnion, and with *Ninny's Well* (as St Cuthbert is with *Cuddy's Well*). It was St Brandon who gave his name to Brandy's Well and therefore to that otherwise inexplicable farm near Capheaton, *Brandywell Hall*.

As our ancestors used the word Well to describe almost any kind of Spring or Stream, however large, it is a little difficult to distinguish one from the other without a knowledge of the exact location. In so far as these Wells were in fact Springs, they were concerned in a good deal of 'well-worship' in pre-Christian times under the impression that they were the abode of spirits to whom prayers should be said. This was particularly the case with the Scandinavians whose influence can be traced at Chirnells near Whittingham. The fact that there now exist *Red Chirnells*, *Black Chirnells* and *Blue Chirnells* points to a distinction between roofs as in the case of Red Row (now the *North Farm*) and *Black Row*, at Throckley and, indeed, *Red Row* near Broomhill. Chirnells itself was still known in 1178 as Childerlund, the Children's Grove, which later became Chirlund.

Where the Children came into the picture is anyone's guess but these people had some unpleasant habits, so it is to be hoped that they did not sacrifice children to the Well Spirit. Later on, this place, or another not far away, was known to the Ogle family as Kirlne House (denoting a Church) and it rather looks as if the reputation of a 'holy' place persisted long after Christianity was introduced and that the newer faith was virtually superimposed on the older. On the other hand it seems just as probable, that the Cyric leah, or Clearing with a Church which is represented by Kirlne, was in reality *Chirm*, the farm near Forestburngate.

In any case, the spirits which inspired this well-worship seem to have survived into the new era in the shape of 'haunts'. It may be going a little too far, however, to say, as one of our historians has, that 'the White Lady, generally called the Silky in Northumberland, is unquestionably a personification of the great Scandinavian Goddess Freyja'.

With the spread of Christianity there also appeared the Holy Wells. At *Holywell*, for instance, near Seaton Delaval there were several Chemical, or Healing Springs, one of them dedicated to St Mary. As often as not the Old English 'halig' has persisted so that fifteen hundred feet up in Hexhamshire there also appears *Hallywell*.

Perhaps the best known of all is at *Holystone* in Coquetdale where a Stone commemorates the fact that Paulinus baptised three thousand at the spring that afterwards bore the name of St Ninian. This must have been quite an occasion when one considers that the total population of the county at that time must have been considerably less than ten thousand in all. Later still, a Priory to house six or eight Nuns was built here; hence *The Priory Farm* and the change of name to the Ladies' Well.

Near *Shiremoor* (the Marsh forming the boundary of Tynemouth Shire) is *Holystone Farm* where once a Stone marked another boundary; this time between the lands of Tynemouth Priory and those of **Long Benton**, the Homestead or Farm where Beans were grown.

In addition to the many stream-names that are distinguished by the ending 'well', there are a great number of variations on the same theme. For instance there is the Slow-running Stream, generally passing through marshy ground, known as a Letch, as in *Gorfen*

Letch, near Longhorsley, which takes its name from a Marsh where Gorse grows. Or there is *Queen's Letch* where Queen Margaret and her son are supposed to have rested after the battle of Hexham Levels during the Wars of the Roses.

Another name for a stream was a Rithe which appears in *Ritton*, the Homestead by the Stream. And then there is *Deadwater*, called after the river that has its origin in a sulphur spring in a Scottish bog and, according to Hodgson, the County Historian, 'runs in the most sluggish manner along a level plain, from which circumstances it is called Dead Water'.

If the stream is really small, it will probably be described as a Sike. *Longsyke*, for example, lies by the Lengthy Caw burn, while *Churnsike* is distinguished by an old Celtic river-name which is fairly common throughout England and appears for instance in Cirencester. A rare instance of the Scandinavian equivalent (so far as Northumberland is concerned) is to be found in the Foul, or Dirty, Stream at *Fulbeck*, near Morpeth.

But the commonest of all, of course, is the Burn which turns up in a great number of our place names. If a settler chose a place where there was a Pool in the Burn it might be known as *Powburn* or even *Kettleburn* (from 'cietel', a cauldron). If in a Meadow, it might be called *Medburn* or if the stream was dug out, or ditched by man, *Ditchburn*. There might even be stepping-stones in which case it would be *Hipsburn*. A Hill by a Stream becomes *Burnlaw*, Land partially Surrounded by it *Burnholme*, and a House in its Enclosure by the Stream, *Bruntoft*. *Whemleyburn* describes a Snug Clearing while *Forestburngate* is the Gap where a Burn (admittedly) emerges from Rothbury Forest, but one which probably takes its name from 'fearr-steg'—a Path trodden by Bulls.

Or, of course, a place might be named after the settlers who lived by the Burn, and so Lilla's name is perpetuated in *Lilburn*, as well as in *Lilswood*, which was called after the thane who saved King Edwin's life at the expense of his own. Sigemund was the originator of *Simonburn* and Cilla of *Chibburn* for, like the Italians, our ancestors seem to have altered the sound of the letter 'c' before certain consonants. Here at Chibburn was a Preceptory, a name usually given to a house or college belonging to one of the Militant Monastic orders; in this case the Knights Hospitallers of St John of Jerusalem (otherwise known as Knights of Malta or of Rhodes).

When all other inspiration failed the place could even be called *Close-a-burns*, a name applied in real life to a farm literally Enclosed by Burns. What a pity it is that there is no farm named after the *Whapweasel Burn* or *Manywaygoburn* (a name described by Mawer as 'corrupt beyond recovery').

Where there are Streams there must also be Mouths, such as *Smalesmouth* where the North Tyne is joined by the Smales burn, the stream that makes its way through the Small (in other words Narrow) part of a valley and which gives its name to *Smales*. *Tynemouth* and *Tillmouth* lie at the Outfall of rivers that both derive their name from a Celtic word meaning to Dissolve or Flow.

Rather surprisingly, *Jesmond* turns out to be a frenchified corruption of Yesemuth, the Mouth of the Yese or Ouse Burn, a stream-name that we have already met at Easington and which appears in various forms all over England. To the Celts it meant Rushing Water.

We have already heard a good deal about Haughs and Hopes in Northumberland, largely because the land in question tends to be more fertile than the soil above it, and this is especially true, of course, of Haughs. There is another reason, namely that both lie close to water, without which no settlement could exist.

Another Old English word sometimes associated with valleys is 'hwamm'. This meant a Corner or Nook that was Snug in the sense of being protected from the weather. Now *Wingates* denotes a Narrow Gap or Way where the Wind rushes through, and was what one might call a technical expression. *Wingates Whalme*, then, is the Snug Corner protected from the Windy Gap.

Beamwham describes such a place where Trees grow, and incorporates an old word that still survives in the Hornbeam tree and in our description of large pieces of timber. *Whitwham* takes its name from the White grass; *Ulwham* and *Ulgham* from being haunted by Owls. It is an interesting commentary on the way in which pronunciation has remained very much unchanged, while spellings have sometimes taken a curious form, that *Whamlands*, near Whitfield, is always pronounced Holmlands, for this is exactly what it is; namely the Land by the Water Meadows and nothing to do with a 'hwam'.

For some reason the sound 'lin' has always had something to do with water. The Celtic word for a lake or pool survives in the Welsh 'llyn' while our English ancestors called any kind of torrent 'hlynn'. In Northumberland it seems to have meant anything from a Pool to a Waterfall and particularly the latter. Thus *Roughting Linn*, where the Greenridge burn falls thirty feet into a pool below, is the Roaring Torrent and *Linnheads* near *Woodburn* (where the Stream emerged from the Forest) describes a place Above the Weir.

Efforts have been made in the past to connect places like *Linsheeles* and *Linbridge* with Lime trees, which are most unlikely to have grown there. These, then, are the Summer Hut(s) and Bridge by the Pool just as *Linhope* and *Linhaugh* are the Blind Valley and the Low Ground by the same.

A pool left by the tide is known in Northumberland as a Low, hence the same name for a number of tidal streams and particularly the River Low, which not only gave the Farm past which it flows its name of *Lowick*, but also explains *Lowlynn*, with its Waterfall. Yet *The Linnels*, though right on top of the Devil's Water, owes its name by a coincidence not to any pool or torrent but to the fact that Linel originally settled there: it was therefore Linel's (Place).

Then there is that delightful name *Kipperlynn*, with its fishy overtones. It has been suggested that it is derived from the word Kipper which was originally the name of a male Salmon; thus conjuring up a romantic picture of fish leaping up a Waterfall. Alas, the name means nothing of the kind for in 1307 it was Skitterlynn and the real explanation is a Torrent used as an Open Sewer.

When Sir Walter Scott wanted to build himself a mansion he found that the site was known locally as Clarty Hole, so he changed it to Abbotsford. Small wonder then that some occupant of Skitterlynn was moved to do the like with a place that had been named so rudely by others: it was even known for a time as Lindeen. The same might well have happened with *Trickley* (which was known in 1177 as Trikelton, the Homestead that always seemed to be thick with Sheep Dung) if the expression had not subsequently gone out of use. A natural corruption of the original Sock-Peth, the place where there was a Channel draining the Juices of a Midden, has meant that

Soppit has also survived the years while Dunghope, nearby, has disappeared. That this process of bowdlerisation still goes on is shown by *The Bog* recently changing its name to *Brownchester*.

If one cares to look for them, however, there are quite a number of places in the county whose origin is dubious, if not actually dirty. There are three Hortons at least. One, near Lowick was once known, from the name of its owner, as *Horton Turberville* (what a pity it has not retained the name). The second, near Blyth, was *Horton Guyschard*, or *Horton Shirreve* because it was the home of the Shire Reeve or Sheriff, and the third was (and is) *Horton Grange*, originally a Grain Farm of Newminster Abbey. The derivation in each case is the Dirty, or Muddy, Homestead.

Much the same could be said of *Sleekburn*, known in 1050 as Sliceburne, the Muddy Stream, *Slaggyford*, the Muddy Ford and *Slaley*, the Muddy Clearing. *Lough House* is explained by its Lake and Boggy ground gives *Saugh House* and *Saughy Rigg* their names, but *Sparty Lea* has in fact no such connection; being called after the Coarse Rushy Grass that covered the original Clearing. *Sparty Well*, curiously enough, is no relation; the name being derived from a Gushing Spring. *East Flass* is named after a Marshy Pool and *Dirt Pot* near Allenheads and *Foul Potts* near Lambley are both named after muddy Pools. There are no such dirty overtones, however, about *Potland* which simply describes the Land by a Pool.

It must not be thought that *Potts Durtrees* near Otterburn has the same kind of derivation although there have been some odd theories advanced in order to explain the name. Certain facts are clear; namely that in 1275 it appears as Dortrees, that in 1618 Cuthbert Potts and others of that ilk paid rent for land hereabouts at a time when there were two farms here, namely Durtrees and West Durtree, and that in 1663 it was described as 'of Potts'. The theory that the place is named after the ruins of a farmhouse bearing the initials of the Potts family but with only the Doorposts or Doortrees standing is virtually exploded by the name appearing as early as 1275. It is just possible that there is confusion here with the Homestead by the Sharp or Steep Hill, now known to us as *Sharperton*. Here there was known as lately as 1910 to be a ruined house of which only the doorway still remained standing, over which was the inscription 'G.P. E.P.

1675 Roger Potts'. In point of fact the name Durtrees is believed to consist of the Celtic 'dur', meaning Water and the English Trees: therefore the place where Trees grow by the Water.

Nor has *Dryburn* anything to do with 'drit', as dirt was so often spelt (witness our old friend John Dulp-in-the-drit): the burn does literally Dry up. There exists, moreover, another Dry Spot in the Ridge of *Druridge*.

Turning once more from dry to wet, it is worth having a look at the good Old English word 'mor' for this can mean either a Moor, in the modern sense of the word, or a Marsh. The former meaning is probably commoner in Northumberland than in most counties because of the nature of the countryside. It must be acknowledged, however, that in a great many cases we will be talking about land that was previously wet, even if it is now drained. *Old Moor* and *New Moor*, for instance, near Ulgham, originally formed part of Pend-more, or Penda's Swamp, which drained into the Potland Burn, so called because it carried the water from the various Pools.

Denwick (meaning the Farm in the Valley) has given its name to a Common out of which a number of farms have been carved that are anything but wet. *Goldenmoor*, probably takes its name from the Gorse; *Silvermoor* from Whiteish grass, as in the case of *Silver Hill* near Stamfordham, while *Peppermoor* represents that part of the Moor where a Piper lived.

Another farm carved out of the waste is *Renningtonmoor*. One of the bearers of St Cuthbert's coffin, when the monks of Lindisfarne fled before the marauding Danes, was Raegenwald, the son of the man who gave his name to *Rennington*, the Homestead of Raegen's people.

Unlike *Morley Hill*, in all probability the Hill on the Moor, *Singmoor*, in Coquetdale, is definitely a moor in the modern, that is to say dry, sense of the word but its derivation is obscure. The most likely explanation is that it has the same meaning, though it is to be hoped, not the same associations, as Broadmoor. On the other hand *Carter Moor*—now two farms—is a low-lying stretch of ground between the Pont and the Blyth. It first appears in history as Kartram Moor in 1613. Perhaps it is the same place that was earlier mentioned as part of the Manor of Eland and known to the scribes as La Charnet. A document of 1280 was witnessed by Robert (the) Carter of Ponteland, so this was probably Carter's Moor.

Murton and *Murton House* are Homesteads, and *Morwick* the Farm, by the Swamp. The same meaning of 'mor' is to be found in *Deanmoor*—the Swamp in a Valley. By the same token *Deanraw* is the Row of Houses and the *Deanhams* (of which there are at least two) the Villages, in a Valley.

Finally there is *Moory Spot*, which overlooks *Prestwick Carr*, the Swampy ground which, when drained under an Enclosure Act, gave its name to *Carr Grange* and *Carr House*. In winter the Carr used to be completely flooded while in summer it contracted into four meres or pools known as the Black, Seggy, Link (or Cloggy) and Moory Spot Pools. From the last, and nearest, of these Moory Spot takes its name.

The word Carr, so far as it affects the place names of Northumberland, is almost impossible to translate unless one knows the situation of the place in question. Sometimes, it arises from an anglicised version of the Scandinavian 'Kiarr' as in *Walker*, the Marsh by the (Roman) Wall: more often it is used to describe a Peat Bog. In that case the meaning will be the same as if it were called a Moss, for example *Kemping Moss*, which was once Centwine's Fen. *Moss House* and *Mosswood* have the same purport while *Hall Peat Moss* signifies a stone-built house by such a Bog. A Mire, as in *Charlton Mires* or *Mirehouse* does not necessarily contain peat.

There is, however, a much older meaning of the word Carr, which was borrowed by our English forebears (this time from the Celtic) and signifies a Rock. This is the explanation of *Carr Houses* and *Carr Hill*, on the Military Road.

The summer retreat of the Priors of Hexham Abbey took the form of a visit to their farm at Karrau Sid, the Hillside that probably took its name straight from the Celtic 'carreg', meaning Rocks. It is now known as *Carraw*, while the Roman Camp of Procolitia earned the name of *Carrawburgh*, the Fort by the Rocks.

The old spelling of *Amble* was (rather charmingly) Annebelle, that is to say Anna's Promontory (or Bill, as in Portland Bill) and off the coast lie the *Bondi Carrs* or Rocks of Bundi (a Scandinavian). Not only have these rocks caused the wreck of a great number of ships but they have also given their name to the farm of *Bondicar*.

It might be thought that *War Carr* meant 'Beware of the Bog' (which has a familiar ring) but the derivation is much more complicated than that. In 1479 the records of Hexham Abbey show four pieces of land near Thirlwall. These were Warde-snak-colfe, Wyrch-snake-colfe, Werth-maybe and Wyrth Keryne (which became War Carr) and it is anybody's guess now what any or all of these weird names signified.

Not far away was another piece of land known as Whirl-cou-a-calfe. This could be Old English for the 'wherfel', Whorl or Circle, (perhaps the remains of a Roman turret?) just large enough for a Cow and Calf. There should therefore be no need to look to the Celtic for an explanation.

The solution of War Carr is taken a step further by the existence of a Watch Hill nearby, now known as *Wardrew*. A state of vigilance against the Scots, or for the matter of that, against anyone else, demanded Watch and Ward, that is to say a state of wakefulness ('waecce') by night and of looking out in a specified direction ('weard') by day. The hints of various kinds of watchfulness that these extraordinary names convey tempt one to think that the meaning of Wyrth Keryne, and therefore of War Carr, is The Watch Rocks.

When a Scottish Historian wrote many hundreds of years ago 'the Scots ... summoned the boors (peasants) who ... made such holes and gaps thro' the wall as they might readily pass and repass thro' and thus settled themselves in England' he was concerned with the time when the Romans had departed and left the inhabitants to deal with their enemies as best they could. The most important of the Gaps he was alluding to was where the Wall was Thirled, or Pierced, at *Thirlwall,* a place that gave its name to a family which though it never held a barony, seems always to have used the title of Baron; hence *Baron House*.

The word Thirl still survives as a description of the gap in a moorland fence through which sheep can pass. *Thirlings*, near Milfield, however, must have been Land where the occupier was 'thirled' or Bound to grind his corn at a specified Mill. Using the word in the same sense of Binding or Enclosing, we find Hodgson referring to the Wall itself as the Thirlwall.

All this, however, is a far cry from the Moors, Swamps and Bogs of Northumberland. One of the few Bogs in the county that are comparable to Prestwick Carr is *Newham Bog*, as famous for its wild plants as the Carr used to be for its bird life. This stretch of Peat by the New Village, carries the main railway line from London to Edinburgh, the only satisfactory foundation for which proved to be bales of wool that virtually floated on the water. *Newham Hagg* takes its name from the Drier Peat standing out from the Bog.

This word Hagg can bear a number of different meanings; one of them being a 'Projecting Mass of Peat', another a Wood marked for Cutting and a third a Wood used for Sheltering cattle. It is the second or third of these meanings that seem most applicable to the Hill of *Hagdon*, near Alnwick, to *The Hagg* (once Piperdean Hagg) near Carham and to *Hagg House* near Bedlington.

Elsewhere in the county the word Bog is used as an alternative to Carr in a number of cases, some of which we have already met. *Harrobog*, for instance, is so named because of some Holy Place, while *Hunger Bog* was just an indication of desperately Poor Land.

A chapter that has dealt with dirt, mud and wet, would hardly be complete without some allusion also to crime. *Poddy Bank*, in Hexhamshire, was originally Podsbank, the Hill of the Poid or Ruffian; a word which might possibly explain that strange name for the stones near Cambo that are known as 'Poind and his Man'. Nowadays a Wretch is a 'person without conscience or honour' but the Old English 'wrecca' from which the word is derived, had a more specialised meaning so that *Ratchwood* probably denotes the Wood and *Ratcheugh* the Spur of a Hill, where an Outlaw lived.[6] *Rushycap* and *Rashercap*, however, are probably both named after Rush-infested Hills.

The use of the word Crook to describe a Swindler is very modern indeed so that it is entirely coincidental that it is in the sense of Bent (or Winding) that we use it in our place names. Thus *Crookham* is the village by a Bend (in the Till) and the same kind of explanation applies equally to *Crooks* and *The Crook* and the Winding Valley of *Crookdean*, but at *Crookhouse* (in 1323 just Le Croukes) there is no

Bend in the Bowmont Water so the meaning must be, in this case, a Crooked Piece of Land.

With *Cruelsyke* we return to the idea of a winding waterway. Though it was known on at least one occasion to 'run red with Scottish blood' the Little Stream takes its name not from any particular savagery but from its Crooked Course. *Crooked Oak* which stands in a violent bend of the Derwent has been known in the past as Crookdale and as Crook Oak and the probability is that it owes its name to a 'Crook(d) Aec', or Oaktree which stands in the Bend.

NOTE

[6] If so, then the fact that both places lie near the Ratcheugh, or Great Whin Sill, is pure coincidence.

CHAPTER 11

No attempt has been made in this book to go back further into the history of Northumberland than the Celts, and for two very good reasons; first that (by definition) so little is known about pre-history and second that, so far as one can tell, it has not affected our place names very much.

This is not, however, to say that the county bears no traces of our more remote ancestors' activities: they are apparent for instance in the strange 'cup and ring' markings on the rocks near Roughting Lynn; on Weetwood Moor and elsewhere. What is more important to the study of place names is the survival of a number of 'menhirs' (a word signifying Long Stones) at Swinburne, in the Coupland Henge and elsewhere. *Threestone Burn House* at Ilderton, for instance, takes its name from the henge, or stone circle nearby.

Outside the farmhouse of *Standing Stone*, at Matfen, stands such a menhir in the shape of a tall, more or less pointed, stone into which are cut a number of deep grooves. Known as the Stobstone, it is reputed to have been used for centuries as a whetstone on which men sharpened their swords. It is possible that the name *Stand Alone,* near Whittonstall, is not so much a pathetic reminder of the place's lonely situation as an indication of the existence of another such single stone, or monolith.

In the days when gate-posts, or gate-stoups as they are known in Northumberland, were invariably made of stone, their production was a flourishing industry: hence *Goatstones* (once Gatestones) near Simonburn, and *Stoop Rigg* only a mile or two away. 'Stoppa' was the Old English word for a Bucket so that it would be tempting to describe *Stouphill,* near Alnwick, in terms of Jack and Jill. Reason, however, forbids and it is almost certain that this is another place from which Stone Gateposts were quarried. The *Bendor* stone, after which the farm was named, and which marks the battlefield of Homildon Hill might have been another of the same sort.

Dorothy Forster, famous for the rescue of her brother Tom from the Tower of London after the '15, came from *Adderstone*, as well as the blacksmith who helped her. The name, however, has no connection with the 'adderstyens' that fishermen used as lucky charms, thinking that the holes in them had been made by Adders. In fact it was Eadred's Homestead and no more to do with stones than Centwine's Dene (the Valley of the Fenham burn) now known as *Kentstone*. As our old name for an Adder was Ether it might be thought that *Etherstone* might have such an association even if Adderstone had not. Nevertheless this was probably Ethelred's Homestead.

Evistones, near Otterburn, is one of the lost villages of Northumberland. In 1618 it was known as 'Cleughbrey alias Evington' and has been deserted since 1693. The farm of *Cleughbrae* (the Bank of the Ravine) is now incorporated with *Ashtrees* into the Redesdale Experimental Farm.

The Old English word 'fag', meaning variegated or multi-coloured, is the explanation of *Falstone*, known in the past as The Fawstone and even, by some misunderstanding, The Fause-stone. Whether this particular stone was one inscribed by the Romans, a milestone (Roman or otherwise) or a boundary stone is not known.

Fourstones is rather more straightforward for, in a list of boundaries compiled in 1238, appears the following: '... from the stone to the second stone and so to the third stone and so to the fourth stone ...' Again these boundary stones may or may not have been Roman in origin; a doubt which also exists in connection with *Leaguer House* near Whitchester. This is just too far away from the Wall to make it likely that the place is named after a Roman Milestone. It is much more likely that the name denoted land that was Fallow, just as *Layside* probably describes a similar Hillside.

Settlingstones is another deceptive name. In 1353 there is mentioned one Hugh of Sadelyngstanes. Now anyone riding along the old Stanegate—the Paved Road that connected up the administrative areas of the Romans behind the Wall—would have to climb Grindon Hill. There is no doubt at all that this was the place where the traveller got back into the Saddle after leading his horse up the slope.

> *Word went east and word went west*
> *Word is gone over the sea*
> *That a Laidley Worm in Spindlestone Heugh*
> *Would ruin the North Countree.*

There is no need here to dwell in detail on the famous ballad about the loathsome serpent into which the Princess of Bamburgh Castle was turned by her wicked stepmother, except to draw attention to the stone to which Childy Wynd tied his horse when he confronted the Worm. 'Childe' was a normal term for a youth of noble birth aspiring to knighthood and this particular example was the Princess' brother. The Pillar of Whinstone to which he tied his horse was presumably the same 'spindle' that gives its name to *Spindlestone Heugh*, the second word describing, of course, the Spur of a Hill on which it stands.

The last 'stone' with which we are concerned at the moment is *Featherstone* which in 1215 appears as Fetherstanhalcht, hence the family name of Featherstonehaugh. This was the Low Ground by the River where there was a Fetherstan, in other words a 'cromlech' or 'tetralith' consisting of three uprights and a headstone, which must have looked very much like three giant cricket stumps with the bails on. This name, then, should serve as yet another reminder of prehistory.

It is pretty certain that the same word 'fether' meaning Four, appears in *Featherwood* (near Rochester) but in what sense is not so clear. The point is that, before the coming of the Normans, our word for a forest was 'wud' and the meaning of Wood in most place names is either Forest or Part of a Forest. Four Forests, as a name, does not really make sense but, if it is of comparatively late origin, there is no reason why it should not mean Four Woods, as in the case of Carraw where in 1479 there was a 'pasture called Fethrechawe (Four Copses)'.

There are, of course, a great number of place names in the county in which the word Wood occurs. *Sidwood* for instance is on a Side or Slope and *Lipwood* on a Steep Slope while *Evenwood* is Level and *Weetwood* Wet. The reason for the latter name is not far to find for the bog of *Bannamoor* (the Murderous Swamp?) was not drained or enclosed until well in to the eighteenth century. It was, of course, quite normal in Northumberland to talk of 'weet' for wet. Returning for a moment to the Laidley Worm we find that

> *Lady Helen sat in Spindlestone Heugh*
> *With silk upon her feet:*
> *The seams were sewn wi' cloth of scarlet*
> *To keep them fraw the weet.*

The word might be thought to appear again in *Weetslade* but there is a corruption here and the name actually describes a Valley with Willows.

Woodhorn stands for a Wooded Horn or Point of Land while *Woodhouse Glebe* refers to Church Land near the Wooded Corner. The word Glebe, of course, appears over and over again, denoting fields that were not only owned by the Church but often farmed by the Priest or Parson. In medieval times, for instance, it was quite normal for the incumbent himself to farm forty to sixty acres in a period when the word 'farm' normally stood for thirty; and even to rent further land, so that he probably knew at least as much about agriculture as his parishioners.

Anything that was isolated, single or separated from the rest our ancestors designated 'an', meaning One or 'ana' meaning Lonely. So *Wanwood Hill* describes an Isolated Wood, that is to say one that was not part of the forest; *Wandon* is the Lonely Hill and *Ancroft* a Little Field Separated from the rest of the Homestead or even from the Toft to which it belonged. *Annstead* is therefore much more likely to be the Lonely Steading or Farm than it is to commemorate any particular female.

Then there are the Homesteads in the Wood, giving us names like *Witton* (Wood-tun) and *Wittonstone*. Roger Thornton who died in 1429 was Lord of Witton. He was also the son of Roger Thornton, the Dick Whittington of Newcastle.

> *At Wesgate came Hodge Thorneton in,*
> *With a hap and a halfpenny in a ram's skin.*

Longwitton, then, is self explanatory as is *Netherwitton*, meaning the Lower Witton, just as *Netherton* and *Nedderton* mean a Lower Homestead.

Another common word used by our forefathers for a Wood, or sometimes for a Wooded Hill, is exemplified by *Hirst* and *Longhirst*, the Wood and the Long Wood respectively. A Holt, also meaning a Wood, is a comparatively rare word in the North but *West Nichold* may possibly describe a New Wood while the word Brake, meaning a thicket, appears in *The Breaks*.

Finally there are the Shaws or Copses, such as *Shaw House, High Shaws, Stagshaw* and *Buckshaw* (meaning very nearly the same thing), *Branshaw* which is almost certainly Steep, and *Hanging Shaw* which is Sloping. *Lordenshaws* is said to be a corruption of Lower Dene Shaw(s) while *Shawdon* is the Valley with a Copse.

As has been said elsewhere, trees played a very important part in the life of the early settlers. It would be surprising, therefore, if they had not used the different kinds of tree that they discovered to designate their Clearings. In fact most of the common trees have found their way into the place names of Northumberland, with the exception of the Sycamore which is an importation.

Alders are represented by the Clearing of *Alloa Lea*, by *Allery Bank*, by *Allerwash*, a name that describes the Soil left by the River where Alders grow, and also by *Elrington* which is the Homestead by the Alders and nothing to do with the Sons or people of anybody. Yet *Allerdean* (near Ancroft) also known as Allerburn, which might well be thought to have a similar derivation, is the Valley where Aelfhere lived.

Apple trees explain *Parmentley*, for it was the Clearing where Pearmains were to be found. Another place where they apparently grew was *Palm Strothers* which introduces yet another word for a Bog, this time one that is covered by Scrub.

There is only one other name (except perhaps Orchardfield) that is positively identifiable with Apple trees and that is *Apperley Dene* which in 1201 was known as Appeltreley or the Clearing in which Apple trees grew. There are, however, two other names, in the shape of *Moss Petrell* and *West Petrel Field*, which have so far defied translation. Other pieces of land, no longer identifiable, have been described as Apiltrelaicrok and, what is even more apposite, Apetreley. Considering the standard of our ancestors' spelling it does not seem unreasonable to conjecture that these two farms were once the Apple tree Clearing by the Bog and the Expanse of Land where Apple trees grew.

In 1160 Eskinggeseles appears; in other words the Summer Hut(s) on the Grassland where Ash Trees grow, now known as *Eshells*. The Glade where the same kind of trees were to be found has now become *Eshott*.

It should come as no surprise to find that *Espley* was Asp-leah, or the Clearing with an Aspen tree, for the word Aspen is really an adjective despite its constant misuse.

Beeches and Beechen places are commemorated by *Bitchfield*, *Bockenfield* and *Bogangreen* which all have much the same meaning and by *Bewclay* which is the Cliff or Slope, with Beeches growing on it.

Birches, in a county with a great deal of rough and sometimes boggy land, crop up comparatively often. *Light Birks* is an allusion to Little Birches, *Birkshaw* to a Birch Copse and *Birkenside* to a similar Slope. *Wheelbirks* provides another instance of the old word for a Whorl or Circle, in this case, of Birches, and *Birkhott* re-introduces Hott, our own rendering of Holt to signify a Clump of Trees, which also explains *The Hott Farm* and *Hotbank*.

When Thomas Bewick, the great engraver, wrote of 'the place of my nativity' he mentioned that 'the dean was embellished with a number of cherry and plum trees', so *Cherryburn* may be taken literally. Bird Cherries give *Hackford* its name, yet *Hack Hall* is probably called after the 'haca' or Bend in the Seaton burn.

The Ellern ford, or Ford where Elders grew, has become *Elford* and the Homestead by the Elders, *Ilderton*, while Elms are recognisable only in the Clearing of *Embley*.

On the other hand Hazels seem to have had quite an influence on our place names. Hazeldean has been explained earlier and Hazlerigg we shall meet again. *Hesleyside* denotes a Hill side, *Hesleywell* a Spring and *Hesleyhurst* a Wood, where Hazels grow. It is even possible that *Helsay* was once Haesel-Hoh, the Heel of land covered by Hazel.

Holling Hill, Hollin Green and *The Hollins* (like *Hulne Park*) were all named after Holly Trees. Furthermore there are a number of Mounts which for some obscure reason have a similar derivation. *Mount Hooley* (Whittingham) *Mount Huly* (Matfen) and *Mount Hooly* (Beal) are therefore not so Irish as they sound. The parentage of *Mount Healey* near Rothbury, however, seems to be rather mixed for old maps show at different times (and admittedly in slightly varying locations) Mount Slowly, Holling Hill, Healey and Mount Healey. Taking an average, as it were, it seems reasonable that the original was High-Law and that the Hill has been elevated by time in the same way as *The Mountain Farm* in the Vale of Whittingham. At the time of the '15 the latter place was farmed by George Morrison, suspected like most of his neighbours of being a Jacobite, and was described as Mountain-of-ye-Clay.

The valley where Lime trees grow is now known as *Linden*, and Plum trees grew by the burn that rises at the Buttery Well on Alnwick Moor, thus explaining *Plundenburn*. The Copse from which *Pundershaw* took its name also probably contained wild Plums.

When Swinburne wrote:

> *On Aikenshaw the sun blinks braw*
> *The burn rins blithe and fain.*
> *There's nowt with me I wadna' gie*
> *To look thereon again.*

he was really alluding to Oak trees, for *Aikenshaw* describes an Oak Copse just as *Akenside* (and, incidentally, *Akeld*) describe Slopes with Oaks on them. *Acton* is really Ac-Den, the Valley of Oaks, and *Eachwick* the Farm with Oaks on it.

Hawksteel, moreover, has nothing to do with birds. In 1679 it was described as The Hoaksteel—the Steel, or Projecting Ridge, where Oaks grew. Oaks also covered the Hills of *Knock Law* and *Knogley* and gave their name to the Summer Hut of *Knock Shield*. *Acomb*, wherever it appears, just means At the Oaks.

There is a tradition that the name *Sillywrea* means Happy Nook, or Corner, and this is by no means unreasonable for, to our forefathers, Silly meant Innocent or Happy. It must be admitted, however, that were it not for this local association it would be difficult to avoid explaining it as the Nook where Sallows or Shrubby Willows grow.

Except for *Trewick*, which denotes the Farm by a Tree, that leaves us only the all-pervading Thorn tree, or bush, to consider. Beginning with the Thorntons (Homesteads by the Thorn trees) there are the Demesne Farm of *Thornton Mains* near Norham, and the three Thorntons near Hartburn. Years ago these were known as East and West Thornton and Neshow (the Nose-shaped Spur of the Hill). East Thornton became *Needless Hall*, presumably because it provided such a Good Living; *West Thornton* remained as it was and it was almost certainly Neshow that, when it passed to the Knights Templars, became *Temple Thornton*.

Thorneley used to be known as Thornelawe, the Hill with Thorns and *Thornbrough* the Stronghold by the Thorn bushes. *Thornham Hill* was the Village by the Thorns and *Thornington* the Homestead of the People who came from such a place, while *Thornley Burn* and *Thorney Haugh* took their names from the Clearing and Low Ground where Thorns grew. *Keenley Thorn*, moreover, signifies the Thorn trees by the Clearing where Cena lived; that is to say the same person (or his namesake) that gave his name to the Hillside of *Keenleyside* and the Stream at *Keenleywell House*.

Thorngrafton denotes the Homestead by the Thorn Graf, Grove or Thicket and *Bythorne* just means By the Thorn, but with *Thorhope* (in Knarsdale) we start on three names which are not quite so obviously connected. In this case the heathen god is in no way involved and the name denotes the Blind Valley where, once again, Thorns grow, just as *Turney Shields* is likely to have started life as the Thorny Shielings or Summer Huts. *Caistron*, moreover, has come a long way since it was described in 1160 just as Cers, meaning a 'carse' or Scrubby Marsh, rather like a Strother but probably derived from the same word as Carr. By 1244, however, the place was known as Kersthirn, the Marsh with the Thorn bushes.

Whickhope (like Whittonstall) is named after Quicks or Thorns which in this case seem to have been a feature of the Blind Valley. Presumably these were the natural ingredient of the Hedges that figure in certain place names. *Windyhaugh*, for instance, is not named after a Haugh but was originally Windyhege, that is to say land enclosed by a Hedge but in a Windy Spot. Neither is the *Heigh*, also near Alwinton and for some reason pronounced Hythe, anything to do with a Heugh but is another Hedged Enclosure, perhaps of Scandinavian origin.

Hedgeley, has a different derivation again for in 1150 it is described as Hiddesleie, or Hidda's Clearing.

Hazon has been the subject of a good deal of speculation because the name has so often been spelt Hay-sand. A literal interpretation, however, does not make sense. A more informative spelling has been that of 1170 which was Heisende and there is little doubt that the correct explanation is Hedge's End or, better still, the End of a Hedged-in Enclosure.

One reason for the confusion must lie in the fact that a Hedge used often to be known as a Hay. On the other hand there are a number of places which can be taken more literally. One of them is *Haydon Bridge*. It was of this place that a nineteenth-century historian of the county wrote in a frenzy of ecstatic punctuation 'Of the commodious and busy station of the railway, I can only say, that as my pen approaches the subject, I find it all too elegant. . . .' The name signifies the Valley where Hay is made.

Hayleazes, which lies between the East and West Allens, commemorates the Common Hayfield of the Village and *Low Haber*, not far away, probably the Hill where Hay was made. Another Allendale farm bears the deceptively familiar name of *Hayrake*, in one of whose fields there used to stand a stone with the inscription 'Here lyeth the body of Thomas Williamson who suffered 10 years imprisonment on truth's acount and the non-payment of tithe . . . 1690'. He must have been a pretty obstreperous customer to deserve so harsh a fate. This name could have been difficult in that the word Rake (from 'hraece' a throat) was often used to describe a pass or gap in the hills so that it would be quite feasible for this to be the High Pass. Alternatively a Rake could mean an Expanse, a Road, or indeed anything that you could range over, so that the term 'sheep-rake' still persists. In point of fact a Hayrake was a technical term for an Outlying Meadow, an explanation which may also apply to *Rake House*, near Shiremoor, where there would have been an Outlying Field belonging to the village.

CHAPTER 12

Anyone taking a look at Northumberland in the thirteenth century would probably have noticed little difference in the two hundred years or so since the Conquest. The countryside would still have given the impression of a great forest interspersed with fairly extensive areas of farmland and undrained marsh, and fringed by tracts of hill and moorland. The inhabitants of a fair sized village (where such a thing existed) would consist of the Lord of the Manor, two or three Free Tenants, a couple of dozen Villein Farmers and perhaps eight cottagers. Most of the population, however, would be living either on the few isolated farms or in a township that had started out as a 'tun' or homestead and had failed to achieve the dignity of a village. These townships, divided into 'farms' of about thirty acres, were the basis in very many cases of the much larger farms that we know today, and were referred to as Towns.

Indeed the devastation wrought by the Normans in Northumberland, as a result of the resistance that its inhabitants put up, had left so much starvation and misery in its wake that there probably remained for several generations insufficient people to create any sizeable centres of population.

Newcastle was beginning to grow round the Castle built by William Rufus. Berwick had come a long way since it was just the Barley Farm while Hexham and Tynemouth were already important on acount of their Priories and *Alnwick* (once just the Farm on the Aln) because of its Castle. What the Murder Path was that gave *Morpeth* its name is now lost in the mists of antiquity: in any case the place could not have been, at this date, of any great size. *Blyth, Ashington* and *Wooler* would have been little more than names—in other words Blithmuth (the Mouth of the River of that name), the Valley of Ash trees and the Hill Overlooking a Stream.

In spite of first appearances, however, forest clearance had been proceeding steadily and farms were beginning to extend further up the hills. On open land, fields were often marked out by walls built of stones that were gathered nearby; the actual line of the walls being dictated more often than not by the position of rocks which it was too difficult to move. Such walls also proved necessary to prevent boundary disputes resulting from the increasing number of Granges created by the different Abbeys, not so much in the form of Grain farms but of Sheep-runs on the fells and moors.

Where walls were not convenient for the purpose of enclosing land, an embankment was often used, known as a 'dic' or dyke, meaning something that has been 'digged'. Further south, and apart from such defensive works as Offa's Dyke and the Devil's Dyke, it was the part dug out that came to be known as a Dyke whereas, in Northumberland, the original meaning of the word persisted. It is the bank formed from the spoil taken out of the ditch that is still known as a Dyke or, when surmounted by a hedge, as a Dyke-back.

These early dykes or embankments, some of which date back to Celtic times, should not be confused with the banks thrown up during the sixteenth century as defences against the Scots. These were the result of orders given by the Wardens of the Marches, who controlled the English side of the Border, to the effect that 'portions of land convenient for tillage, meadows or grazing should be enclosed in ditches 5 quarters in breadth and 6 in depth, double set with quickwood and hedged about 3 quarters high'.

Whatever may have been the reason for creating dykes in the first place, there is no doubt that they formed important landmarks, for they inspired many of our place names. For instance the farm that started life as Swynleys, meaning the Clearing(s) where Pigs were kept, became by the fourteenth century the Shielings by the Clearing and finally Shield Dykes.

Near Busy Gap, 'one of the nicks in the ridge of basaltic rocks supporting the Wall', which was also described in 1600 as 'infamous for robbers', lies Crindledykes, a place that was right in the thick of the thievery that continually went on in that part of the World. So widespread was this marauding that there was trodden a regular 'drove road' through the Gap along which the Scottish cattle could be driven. Those who had 'shifted' them could then find shelter behind the Wall. It was in 1703 that Nicholas Armstrong, 'a notorious thief', of Housesteads, was under sentence of death for armed robbery. He charged William Lowes of Crow Hall with trying to 'dismember their neighbour William Turner of Cringledykes of his tongue and ears'. This grisly operation, however, seems to have met with only partial success for Turner, minus half his tongue and one ear, was still able to give evidence against the self-appointed surgeon.

The name *Crindledykes* means the Circular Bank(s) and there is little doubt that it was inspired by the remains of a Roman Signal Station. It would be tempting to apply the same kind of reasoning to *Round Meadows* in Allendale but it is very much more likely that these were originally the 'rymed' or Cleared Meadows. Another Round (apart from Wheelbirks) is to be found in *Whorlton*, the Homestead built in a Circle, and not to be confused with *Whalton*, the Homestead on an Arched Hill.

The presence of an Earthwork or Embankment, whether intended as a boundary or not, has inspired the name of a number of places; among them the Row of Houses at *Dyke Row*, the Terminal point at *Dyke Head* and the Corners at which stood *Dyke Nook* and *Dyke Neuk*. The place that was known in 1303 as Heygham-in-Milburne, or the High Village, is now *Higham Dykes. Pike Dyke Neuk* was probably such a Corner where a man called Pike lived, like his name-sake in the Hollow known as *Pike's Hole*. Normally, however, Pike meant a Peak as in *The Pikes*, so that *Pigdon* is the Peaked, or Conical, Hill.

A Nook, moreover, did not always denote a Corner. *The Nook* near Widdrington, for instance, is called after a 'Knoc' or Hillock. The place was once known as St John's Land, implying a connection with the Knights Hospitallers of St John at Chibburn Preceptory.

If the bank was a Dyke, then the part from which the soil was 'digged' was the Ditch, hence *Detchant*, the Ditch End and *Dissington*, the Homestead of the People who lived by the Ditch—in this case the one running along the north side of the Roman Wall which passed just south of what is now South Dissington.

A smaller ditch would be a Channel or Kennel. The former is to be found in *Channelwell House* in Hexhamshire, whose name probably denotes a Stream running through a Channel. A Kennel is an alternative form of the same word meaning, in particular, a Gutter. Thus in the days when refuse and sewage were thrown into the city streets it was into the Kennels at the side that they found their way, for there were no pavements. *Low Dog Kennel* near Widdrington, then, would have been the Channel where Docks (or possibly Water lilies) grew.

In the case of *Moss Kennels* the explanation is less straightforward. Nearby are the remains of a hypocaust (the hot-air supply for a Roman bath-house) and this may very well have been mistaken at one time for a Kiln. The supposition that this may have been the origin of Kennel in this case is strengthened by the appearance of a hill, on Armstrong's partly illustrated map of 1769 marked Kennel Hill and bearing on it what looks like a Kiln, though this was in a different part of the county. On the other hand, quite apart from the Vallum which runs along the Roman Wall, there must have been a Channel bringing water to the bath-house and this surely provides the correct derivation for the name of a place that adjoins the Moss or Bog that forms the bed of an ancient lake.

Nevertheless a Lime Kiln does feature in no less than three of our place names; in *Kilnpit Hill* from which a southerner driving north obtains his first unforgettable view of Northumberland; in *Kilham* (originally known as Kylnum, or At the Kilns) and, surprisingly enough, in *Lincoln Hill* near Humshaugh which is a straightforward corruption of Limekiln Hill.

There was, of course, another method of enclosure besides Hedges (dealt with in a previous chapter), Walls and Dykes, and that was a Fence, which might either be woven or plaited as at Plashetts or some kind of post-and-rails affair. Nevertheless such names as *Swarland Fence*, where the land was 'swaer', or Heavy to plough, *Stanton Fence* where there was a Homestead on Stony Ground, *Felton Fence*, where there was a Homestead out in the Open or Field, and *Ulgham Fence*, had a totally different meaning. For instance Roger Bertram referred in 1265 to 'common of herbage in his wood (at Swarland) called Ledefens (le defence) west of Harpetburn'. There seems little doubt that a Defence (or 'defensum' as the scribes had it) was what is now known as a Windbreak though, in the case of Swarland, the trees must have disappeared by the seventeenth century when the place was described as 'moorish ground and grew no corn before Enclosure'.

Nowadays the countryside, as we know it, owes its appearance very largely to man. It is composed to a great extent of man-shaped fields surrounded by man-made hedges and fences, crossed by man-laid roads, decorated with man-planted trees and studded by man-built farmsteads. In the thirteenth century the efforts of man, particularly in Northumberland, must still have appeared puny compared to those of nature. Yet the forests, which were still so extensive, actually provided the raw material for a great deal of what we would now call industry. The Manorial system, for instance, allowed each village well defined privileges in the 'waste' that was common to all, including rights of Housebote, Hedgebote (sometimes confusingly known as Haybote), Cartbote, Ploughbote and Firebote.

All this meant that one might, without hindrance, cut timber to build one's house and mend one's fences, carts, or ploughs and collect firewood. As lately as 1784 we read of 'the owners of the said three tenements' being entitled to take out of the demesnes of Fewster Johnson 'sufficient hedgeboot, stakeboot and rice for the making and amending of hedges and fences'. 'Rice' was brushwood, or something of the sort, from which we get the expression Rice-knife for a Hedge-knife.

But the chief beneficiary was often the Lord of the Manor and even the king. The former would invariably own a Park, consisting partly of pasture, partly of woodland, the whole enclosed by an earth bank (in other words a dyke) on which would stand a wall, wooden fence or palisade. The object of this last was twofold; partly to keep trespassers out but more importantly to keep the deer, which were the principal objects of the chase for which the park was primarily designed, inside. The palisade would be pierced at intervals by solid wooden doors. The King's Park at Wark-on-Tyne, for instance, of which *Park End* marks one boundary, was entered by *Latterford Doors*, called after the Beggars' Ford. It would also have in it 'deer leaps' which were specially constructed as 'one-way valves' allowing the red, fallow and roe deer to jump in but not out.

Some of these medieval parks might be quite small, perhaps a hundred acres in extent. Others were immense and it was not unknown for the great barons to raze whole villages to the ground in order to increase their size. One of the more ambitious parks, or rather hunting forests, must have been the Huntland of North Tynedale which appears in history in 1177, if not earlier, and presumably gave its name to the modern *Huntland*. Here it was that William the Lion of Scotland held (from the King of England) 'one third of Haughton and four shielings within the Huntland of Tindale to ocupy winter and summer as meadow, pasture or arable land'. The said William was in the peculiar position of doing homage for land that was actually in England, namely the Barony of Tindale.

The King's Forests consisted, like anyone else's park, both of woodland and of grass and were jealously guarded. People's dogs had to be 'lawed' or, in other words, have the claws of their front paws cut so that they could not hunt. It was strictly forbidden to damage the deer pasture and no cow could be tethered in the forest. The fences had to be kept in order by the surrounding villagers and it was as serious a crime to kill one of the King's deer as to kill a man. Answerable to the Verderer would be a number of Foresters, now commemorated in the names *Forest Hall*, and *Frost Hall*.

The word 'hall' has been attached to farm names for a variety of reasons. As has already been pointed out, it originally signified a stone house as opposed to one built of timber, mud and turf. Subsequently the word was used to describe anything rather grander than the normal, or even as a kind of wry joke. Many of the places that now rejoice in the name of Hall, however, started life in a much humbler way as a Hill or even a Hole or Hollow.

If there are only a few names connected with Foresters, there are quite a number associated with Hunters, or at any rate Hunting; for example the Huntsman's Corner at *Hunter Crook*, his Stream at *Huntwell*, his Hill at *Hunt Law* and his Summer Hut at *Hunter Shield*. *Hunting Hall* would be where a Huntsman lived while *Hunt Rods* would be his Forest Clearing(s) just as *Summerrods* was the Clearing(s) used by someone only in Summer.

King, Lord and Church; these controlled the lives of the ordinary man in the thirteenth century, as throughout the Middle Ages. We have had a cursory look at the first two; perhaps it is time to examine the effect of the third on the people, and more particularly the place names, of Northumberland.

First let it be said that the visible effects of the Church on the names of our villages and farms is probably less than in most counties. Not for us a Church Fenton or a Zeal Monachorum. Nevertheless there are, in fact, a number of names connected more or less, with the Church.

The Cariteth, famous in the annals of North Tynedale, was known in 1325 as Le Caryte, in other words The Charity, from which it may be fairly assumed that the revenues of the place were devoted to that end. In the same way, but later on, the farm that is now known as *Charity Hall* was given in perpetuity to the poor of Rothbury parish.

Prior Mains, which in 1594 was known as Prior Manor Farm and appears in 1668 as Manner de Prior Rawe, was attached for long enough to Corbridge Rectory, and *Prior Hall* near Cambo probably had a somewhat similar history. Another farm once connected with Trinity Church, Corbridge, and known in the sixteenth century as Chantry Close, is named after a *Chantry* endowed in the thirteenth century by one of the Claverings, Lords of Corbridge, with twenty-four acres of land and certain houses in the Market Place.

Chantries, before their suppression in the reign of Edward VI, were widespread throughout the countryside and were anything but the 'superstitious' foundations that those land owners who coveted their possessions were wont to call them. They were, in fact, chapels suitably endowed with farm land, the revenues of which were devoted to the saying of prayers for the dead, and more particularly for the soul of the benefactor. These chantries, when in the hands of the Church, were very often associated with leper hospitals. Alternatively they might belong to one of the City Guilds, in which case the endowment would go not only towards prayers for the dead but towards the maintenance of bridges, harbours or schools.

Other chapels existed for the benefit of parishioners who lived too far away to attend the Parish Church. One such was the Chapel of Hartington that gave *Kirkhill* its name while *Kirkham*, near West Newton, is the Village where there was once a Priory Church.

Armstrong's map of 1769 shows *Maudlin Farm*, at Warkworth, as being on the 'Bishop of Carlisle's Land'. It must have formed the endowment of a Magdalene, the medieval name for an asylum where prostitutes were collected in order to reform them.

In the twelfth century William the Lion of Scotland granted the Manor of Whitfield to the Canons of Hexham so it is no surprise to find there the *Monk Farm*, with its traces of ecclesiastical architecture and remains of a tithe barn to which the faithful (and others) could bring their tithe at a time when it was always levied in kind. In 1669 the place was known as Westermuncke, having originally been a House of Correction where unruly monks were sent from Hexham Priory. At one time *Chirton* used, to be known as Shire Town, in ignorance of its origin as the Church Homestead, so called because it belonged to the monks—this time of Tynemouth Priory.

Monkseaton was the Homestead by the Sea, which also belonged to the Monks of Tynemouth, but what Monastery owned the Ridge on which *Monkridge* stood is not immediately apparent. The present Monkridge is the farm that used to be known as Overmonkridge. The original (now Monkridge Hall) appears in more than one document as Mounceridge and this may provide a clue to that otherwise inexplicable name, *Mounces* (in North Tynedale). In 1753 it was referred to as Mounces Park and in 1763 as Mouncesknowe. The probability is that the present name is a corruption of Monks' Knowe, or Hillock.

Another slightly mysterious name is *Climbing Tree*. The first part of the mystery is not difficult to solve. The place was originally St Clement's Trees. Now the local abbreviation of Clement is Clim and to clim is to climb, so there you have it. What is not so easy to discover is why it was called after St Clement in the first place. It is to be presumed that the Barkers' Guild of Newcastle had a Chantry here, for St Clement is the patron saint of Tanners (to use the modern word) and there still exist the remains of a Chapel there. Indeed until well into the nineteenth century tanning was the most important industry of Morpeth, and when the town was reputed to have the second biggest cattle fair in England there were ten tanneries working there night and day.

Another saint to be commemorated in the name of a place is St John of Beverley who, in the seventh century, lived in retirement on the spot now known as *The Hermitage* before being called to become Bishop of Hexham. Hence the Parish of *St John Lee*. There is, of course, at least one other place called *The Hermitage*, this time at Warkworth, of which the origin is too well known to go into here.

Then there are the various Hospitals that must have dotted the countryside for, as has already been pointed out, the word applied to almost any kind of shelter intended to benefit body or mind. *Spital* is therefore a fairly common name. At Horsley, for instance, stood the Hospital of St Michael of Welton which was erected where the present farm stands, in order to shelter those who took the waters of the medieval well, and *Spittle Hill* at Mitford commemorates St Leonards Hospital. These would be medical hospitals in the full sense of the word but *Spittleford* probably derives its name from a Ford beside which a Wayfarers' Shelter stood.

In the south, the word Stoke (from 'stock', a Monastery or Holy Place) is comparatively common in such names as Stoke Newington, Stoke D'Abernon and so forth, but in Northumberland it is very rare. The only example that comes readily to mind is *Stocksfield* which takes its name from the Open Expanse belonging to the Holy Place, which must almost certainly have been Hexham Priory. Another example of rather the same kind is *Stiddle Hill* which was once the Stede-hlaw or Hill where there was probably a Place of Worship of some kind.

The Church in medieval times was, of course, by no means a male prerogative and Nuns also have left their mark on the place names of Northumberland, even if there does not seem to be much originality about them. When Roger Bertram gave Baldwine's Wood, near Morpeth, to the Nuns of Holystone it is not surprising that the Ridding, or Clearing, made in it was known as *Nun Riding* and it may well have been the same Nuns who built a Church at *Nunnykirk*. That *Nun Hill* near Belsay and *Nunwick*, with its Lady Well, belonged to some Nunnery is, of course, quite likely but it should be borne in mind that Nunna was not an uncommon name before the Conquest and it is more than probable that Nunwick at least, was originally Nunna's Farm.

To return once more to the Monks, it might be thought that *Bennetsfield*, near Otterburn, took its name from the Benedictines, Bene't being the normal abbreviation of Benedict. There is, in fact, no evidence that this was the case; whereas there is known to have been a family called Beynet or Benet in Newcastle in 1235, if not earlier, and this was probably an Expanse of land in their ownership.

Friars Hall, at Alnwick, used to belong to the Monks of Hulne Priory and *Bamburgh Friars* to the Black Friars. *Bamburgh* itself must be not only the most historic place in Northumberland but perhaps in the whole of England. When first we hear of it, it is the Celtic Dinguardi, a name which is supposed to mean the Citadel of the Games. No wonder that it has ben identified as the Joyous Garde of Arthurian legend.

The ancient kingdom of Northumbria, which stretched from the Humber northwards to the Forth, originally consisted of Deira to the south and Bernicia to the north, the two becoming united at the end of the sixth century. It was in 537 that Ida, the first King of Bernicia, rebuilt as a royal palace the fortification that crowned the rock of Bamburgh, and a later King, Aethelfrith, left it to his widow Bebba: hence the name Bebban-burgh or Bebba's Castle. It might be thought that *Bebside* might have belonged to the same lady: in point of fact this was the Park or Seat of one Bibba, a totally different person.

There are, of course, a number of Crosses in the county, after which farms might reasonably have been named, and these include the Percy Cross at Otterburn, the Steng Cross near Elsdon, Comyn's Cross on Haughton Common and so forth. There are also farms with names like *Crossridge, Cross House* and *Cross Bank* but they are in the wrong places. Some will have been named after Boundary or Roadside Crosses but it seems probable that in the case of others there may never have been a cross and that the name has arisen because that is where the Cultivation Strips of the Town Fields have crossed, or run at right angles to, the normal direction.

Finally there are two Oxford Colleges (at least) which have left their mark on our place names. One is Merton, the owners of the Ponteland living, whom we shall meet again at Embleton: the other is Balliol, represented by *Balliol Farm* at Benton. It was in 1268 that John de Baliol, the holder of the barony of that name, which stretched from Bywell all the way to the Derwent, died. He had already planned the creation of the Oxford College that bears his name but it was left to his widow Devorgilla to found it. Although Benton is not mentioned among the immense possessions of the Baliol family extending, as they did, from Bailleul-en-Vimeu (in Poitou) through various counties of England to the South-West corner of Scotland, the connection is plain.

CHAPTER 13

From Goswick we've geese
And from Cheswick we've cheese,
From Buckton we've venison in store.
From Swinhoe we've bacon
But the Scots have it taken
And the Prior is longing for more.

So runs one verse of 'The Black Sow of Rimside and the Monk of Holy Island'. With *Goswick*, the Goose Farm, and one of the resting places of Charles I and his army on their way to Scotland, we start on a long list of names associated with Birds, Animals, Reptiles and Insects. But we also encounter the 'specialist' farms owned by Monasteries and the larger manors. *Cheswick*, for instance, is the Farm at which Cheese was made, just as the Berewicks that we have already come across, provided Barley. Yet the most common function of a 'wic' was that of a Dairy Farm, and so we get names like *Luddick*, *Prendwick* and *Wintrick* where Ludda, Prend and Wintra milked their cows. And, for the matter of that, Aluborg and Ella, who were respectively (and perhaps surprisingly) a woman and a man who farmed, one at *Abberwick* and the other at *Elwick*. *Anick*, near Corbridge is another of the same kind, and is thought to have belonged to that same Egelwin who was Bishop of Durham about the time of the Conquest. *Keepwick* is the Farm where some kind of Trading was done but *Sledwick* is a corruption of Slidda's Waesse, or Swamp.

Before the Normans arrived, with the manorial system that seems to have been their biggest contribution to the countryside, the greater part of the land in the county, as elsewhere, was held in common by the 'tun' or Township. This had evolved from the original Homestead and the land in question was known as folc-land. An individual might, however, own a certain amount that he could transfer by deed (or book) which was consequently known as 'boc-land'. *Buckton*, seems to have been a Homestead transferred by 'book' and hence its name, which, except in the mind of the poet, has no connection with the kind of Buck that might be expected to provide venison.

Buckton, incidentally, has another claim on our attention for this was where Grizel Cochrane brought off her famous exploit. Her father, Sir John Cochrane, was lying in the Tolbooth at Edinburgh awaiting imminent execution. His daughter, knowing the warrant to be on its way from London, travelled down to Belford where she spent the night. Next day she dressed up as a highwayman and hid in the wood, known to this day as Grizzy's Clump, beside the Great North Road, whence she held up the mail coach, secured the warrant and won enough time for her father's friends to obtain a pardon for him from James II. She must have been a most intrepid character, and the ballad does her no more than justice:

> *The warlocks are dancing threesome reels*
> *On Goswick's haunted Links:*
>
> *On Kyloe's hills there's awfu' sounds*
> *But they frightened not Cochrane's Grizzy.*

With *Swinhoe*, the Spur of a Hill where Swine were kept (or, more probably, where Wild Boar were to be found) we enter into the realm of animals, or at any rate of animals that have left their mark on our place names, beginning with the domesticated ones.

There is little doubt that Bullocks inspired such names as *Bullshill* and The Thicket of *Bullbush* and it is probable that *Bullions* denotes Bullock Pastures. Cows are represented by *Kyloe House* which used to be known as the South Kellawes or Hill(s) where the Kye were turned out. In most of the really old names the word Cow, associated with some kind of building, rarely means what it says. Nevertheless there is evidence that *Cowstands* (possibly Cowsteads to begin with) can be taken literally, while *Cowbyers* has quite an ancient pedigree.

Some time before 1214 Hugh de Bolbec had granted to the monks of Blanchland certain land in the vicinity, but reserved to himself forty acres at Heselwoode together with the right to make a 'vaccarium' or Cow-byre; from all of which the monks were to have the tithe.

Yet there are nearly as many names that look as if they have a connection with cattle, and have not, as there are of the genuine article. Cowpen, for instance, which comes into the story again later, is a good example of the rule just quoted; Bullocksteads is not all it appears to be; *Stirkscleugh* describes the Ravine where Styrcol lived and *Hefferlaw* the Hill by the High, or Upper, Ford. The Hill where Calves were turned out is now known as *Kellah* (like Callerton) and the Clearing or Pasture where they were kept is now *Callaly*.

Historically speaking, it is only a comparatively short while since almost the only draught animals used on the land were Oxen, so it comes as no surprise to find names like *Oxenheugh, Oxcleugh* and *Oxfoot* meaning the Spur of a Hill, Ravine and Ford, respectively, where Oxen were kept or watered.

As might be expected, neither Dogs nor (domesticated) Cats concern us here, except for *Houndalee*. Conceivably it could be the Clearing where Hounds were kept but there seems a fair chance that it is the same place as the ancient Hengandelyes, so often mentioned in the records of the Ogle family. Alternatively, the latter may have been the original of the famous field at the experimental farm of Cockle Park known as *Hanging Leaves*. In any case the meaning is the Sloping Field(s).

Cuddy's Well is not the only place in the county left to remind us of St Cuthbert; nor shall we forget him as long as we affectionately know as a Cuddy the beast that served him so faithfully. *Cuddycotes* at Throckley most likely denotes the Outbuildings where Donkeys were kept (perhaps for work in the pits?) though it is only fair to add that the name has sometimes been spelt Cuttycoat, implying a Ragged Coat in the same way that Cutty Sark meant a Ragged Shirt.

It is not surprising that Horses figure fairly prominently in the place names of Northumberland when one considers that not only did they provide a universal form of transport but also one of the most important sinews of war. Indeed the advent of the Great Horse, specially bred to carry the vast weight of a knight in armour, once had just as revolutionary an impact on warfare as the tank has had in our day.

Before the arrival of the Normans it was already common practice to use for Horse-folds old Roman, and other existing enclosures, so it is no surprise to find a name like *Stotsfold*, near Hexham. It was a Herd or Stud of Horses that was known as a 'stod'; hence also *Studdon Dene*, the Valley by the Hill where Horses ran.

Horsley and *Longhorsley* denote Clearings, and *Horse Gate* a Pasture, where Horses were kept, and *Mares Close* the Enclosure for Breeding Mares. Foals were certainly kept at the Stronghold that gave *Fowberry* its name and it may well be that *Follions* denotes Pastures used for the same purpose.

So far as Pigs are concerned, we have already had a look at Swinhoe (and previously at Shield Dykes). The Swin Burn, which gave *Swinburne* its name, was probably another place where Wild Boar, rather than domestic pigs, drank. Then there are Houxty and Housty which, rather unexpectedly, have different derivations. *Housty*, near Wark on Tyne, is called (perhaps derisively) after a Hogs' Sty while *Housty*, in Allendale, was originally Howsepette, the Path along which Hogs were driven. *Houtley*, on the other hand, is the Clearing where Holte lived.

The surprising thing is that in a county that now has the second largest sheep population in England there are so few names connected with Sheep. Neither Ramshope, as will soon be apparent, or Tuperee or even Ewesley, have any connection with them. *Sheepwash*, however, means exactly what it says and *Lambshield* and *Lambley* denote the Summer Hut and Clearing, respectively, where Lambs were kept.

It is difficult, a thousand years or so later, to take seriously names connected with really wild animals. Ravines frequented by Wolves and Wild Cats are something that one might expect to find in Canada but surely not in this country. Yet, unquestionably, these were what our ancestors found when they settled here, and it is therefore largely a waste of time to look around for people such as Ulfi and Catta in order to explain away some of our place names.

Brocks, in other words Badgers, have left their mark on a number

of farms such as *Eshott Brocks, Longhirst Brocks* and *Brocks Bushes.*
Brockley Hall and *Brockalee* must have been Clearings and *Brockdam,* a Dammed up pool, where they played. It is even possible that
Beavers are represented. Certainly they were known in this country
at the time when so many of our place names evolved, so it may be
that *Bewshaugh* is the Low Ground by the river where Beavers built
their dams.

It would be a great mistake to think that names like Kitty Green,
Kitty Frisk and *Kittythirst* were necessarily (or even probably) connected with Kittens. 'Kitty' denotes, at any rate in Northumberland,
anything Small so that not only is a small cat a kitten but a (small)
wren a Kitty Wren and one's little finger the Kitty Finger. The most
probable explanation therefore of Kittythirst, and possibly of *Kitty
Frisk* also, is a Little Wood. *Kitty Green* (or Kiddy Green), however,
seems more likely to have been the Grassy Place belonging to
Christopher.

But if there are no Kittens, there are at least several Cats. Thus
Catton (once Catteden) was the Valley, *Catcleugh* the Ravine, *Cat-
heugh* the Spur of a Hill and *Catraw* the Row of Houses frequented
by Cats, while *Catless* probably originated as Catlees—the Clearing(s)
where Cats were to be found.

These were not, of course, domestic cats but the wild variety, of
which there were at one time so many that among the Hunt Servants
attached to the Court of the Norman Kings were not only Wolf
Hunters but 'catatores' or Cat Hunters. One of the last haunts of the
wild-cat in England was the Kielder district, and James Hardy had
this to say in 1874. 'An old shepherd, John Hutton, of Peel, who died
only ten or twelve years ago, aged about eighty, used to say that when
he was a young lad the Keilder herds very seldom went to their sheep
without seeing one or more "wulcats". And my own grandfather, a
shepherd, was once worried by a Wulcat in Keilder. The animal
attacked him without provocation, with the utmost ferocity, aiming
at his throat'. With great difficulty grandfather managed to kill the
animal but without the help of his collie he would undoubtedly have
been killed himself, or at least severely mangled—'On being stretched
on the ground after it was dead, it was found to be, for its length and

girth, bigger than the colley—of course it would be shorter in the legs'.

As an important source both of food and sport, deer have inspired a great number of place names in Northumberland, as elsewhere, though *Darlees*, if it means (as seems probable) the Clearing where Deer were to be found, provides the only one where the actual word is used.

Doe Hill surely indicates a place where Fallow Deer were to be found, just as *Roe Hill* was the haunt of Roe Deer. *Rayheugh* (the Spur of a Hill) and *Raylees* (the Clearing) must also have been associated with the same species. *Ray*, on the other hand, has nothing to do with animals, the name meaning At the Water.

Hindley Wrea, the Corner at the junction of the East and West Allens by the Hill where Hinds graze, introduces the Female Red Deer, while the male of the species appears in *Hartburn* and *Hartford*. *Hartley* and *Hartlaw*, also, were named after Hills and *Hartside* after a Hillside, where Red Deer (and particularly Stags) were to be found.

Hardriding is an interesting name for two reasons. The first is that it has nothing to do with Border Forays or anything of the sort, despite the appearance in history of Hardriding Dick, but signifies the Clearing where Harts gathered. The second reason lies in the difference that it throws up between the Scandinavian use of the word Riding to mean (as in Yorkshire) a Third, and the Old English use which describes something that is 'ridded' of trees, the latter being fairly common in Northumberland. *Riding Mill* is another example of the word, while *Old Ridley* and *Ridley Stokoe* illustrate it in the form of a 'rid-leah' or Cleared Pasture. The family of Stokoe which gave the latter its name took theirs from the Spur of a hill where Tree-trunks were piled up.

The Old English 'rod', meaning a Clearing in the Forest, which we have met before in Hunt Rods and Summerrods, is another form of the same word. It is to be found once more in *Roddam*, the place At the Clearings which has, in turn, given its name to the oldest family in Northumberland, and perhaps in England, who claim that they owe their land originally to King Athelstan, quoting an ancient charter to that effect. A rather more modern version is to be found set out in Saxon characters in the Scottish Heraldry—

I King Athelstan give unto thee Pole Roddam
For me and mine to thee and thine
Before my wife Maude, my daughter Maudlin and eldest son
  Henry
And for a certain truth
I bite this wax with my gang tooth
So long as muir bears moss and cnout⁷ grows hare
A Roddam of Roddam for ever mare.

The presence of a Fox-earth, if not the smell of it, seems to have given cause for a certain number of names but in only two or three cases do they incorporate the modern word. Yet as early as 1325 *Foxton* was known as Foxden, the Valley where Foxes roamed, though why they should have frequented the Buildings now known as *Foxhemmels* it is difficult to imagine.

The old word for a fox was, of course, Tod and for its Earth a Tod-hole. *Todridge* therefore is easily explained while *Toddles, Toodles, Todhill* and *Toddle Hill* are all variants of *Todholes*.

Although Moles have played their part in history (for was it not a molehill over which William III's horse stumbled and threw him so that he was killed?) they have left no lasting impression on the names of Northumberland. That is to say if you do not count *Molesdon* from which it was once thought that the Lords of Mitford obtained their crest of three moles. The real derivation of the name, however, is the Valley where Moll settled.

In the last century *Otterstone Lee* near Falstone appears on one occasion as Otterstooles while in 1604 it is spelt—even more surprisingly—Atterstanley, but there is little doubt that the place was the Pasture by the Stones where the Otters played. It may well be that the reference was to the two little islands nearby.

It is not difficult to accept that it is the Stream where Otters abound that has given *Otterburn* its name but it would be a mistake to believe the same of *Ottercops*, if only because the stream in question is five and a half miles away at its nearest point, Girsonfield. In 1265 the place was spelt Altercopes and, even as late as 1635, Attercops. That

the second part of the word is the Old English for Hill tops is un-
questionable. The first part may be Celtic, in which case it might possibly refer to the High Land so that 'cops' was added in ignorance
of its real meaning. Or it may be the Old English 'atter', a spider's
web, a by no means unreasonable explanation when one considers
that Gossamer is quite a feature of the place.

Girsonfield, to which reference has just been made, was originally
the Open Expanse belonging to Greenson. Moreover it was the home
of the 'Three Fause Haa's' who betrayed Parcy Reed to the Scottish
Crosiers.

> *They're stown the bridle aff his steed*
> *And they've put water in his lang gun.*
> *They've fixed his sword within the sheath*
> *That out again it winna come.*

This kindly action of the Halls not unnaturally left poor Parcy at
the Crosiers' mercy.

> *They fell upon him all at once,*
> *They mangled him most cruellie,*
> *The slightest wound might cause his deid*
> *And they hae given him thirty three.*
> *They hackit off his hands and feet*
> *And left him lying on the lea.*
> *'Now Parcy Reed, we've paid our debt;*
> *Ye canna well dispute the tale'.*
> *The Crosiers said and off they rade,*
> *They rade the airt[8] of Liddesdale.*

Polecats are now comparatively rare; yet once they must have been
important enough to suggest a name for *Foumart Law*—the Foul-
martins' Hill.

If it is difficult, after all these years, to imagine Wildcats and Polecats running round the place, how much more so is it to think of
Wolves. Yet the Ravine of *High Wolf Cleugh* as well as *Wolf Hill* and
Wolf Hills serve to remind us that they also were something to be
reckoned with. And not only these for there is also the place that

was known in 1314 as Wulvedon (the Wolf Hill) and in 1439 as Wuldon, which had become by 1477 *Wooden*, a name it still bears today.

Contrariwise, as Tweedledee would have said, *Wooley* denotes the Clearing by a 'well' or Stream. *Cubstocks*, moreover, has nothing to do with either wolves or foxes for it was originally Cybba's Farm, and probably a Dairy Farm at that.

When one of our historians was describing Hexham, he wrote 'How fond must the monks have been of conventual purity and propriety! The hens kept at one end of the town and the cocks at the other! For surely Hencotes and Cockshaw bear some relation to each other'. It would be curious if the birds kept in the Outbuildings of *Hencotes* were *not* in fact domestic Hens but it would be a grave mistake to mix them up with the Pheasants, or more probably Woodcock, that roosted in the Copse of *Cockshaw*. The truth of the matter is that, although *Birdhope* signifies the Blind Valley where Birds sing, the commonest name for a Wild Bird was Hen. And so we find *Hen Hill, Henlaw* and *Henslaw* which all mean much the same thing. *Henshaw*, near Haltwhistle, looks at first sight as if it were another name of the same kind but nothing could be further from the truth. In the twelfth century, the place was known as Hedeweshalch, and referred to the Low Ground by the river where a Heathen lived; in this case a Danish settler.

Game birds (and particularly Woodcock) were likely to be known as Cocks (as in Blackcock today) and so we have such names as *CockLaw, Cockhill, Cockle* (Cockhill) *Park* and *Ulgham Cockles*. Also *Cockley Walls*, called after the Foundations of someone else's house on the Hill frequented by Birds, and *Cockplay* which has nothing to do with cock-fighting but like *Cock Lake*, signifies a place where Grouse play. *Grousehouse* and *Partridge Nest* would appear to be the nearest equivalent among more modern names.

Woodcock have at least two names to themselves in the shape of *Woodcock Hall* and of *Cockrumple*, a name apparently inspired by the likeness of the Land to the Rump of a Woodcock sitting on her nest; 'rumpill' being an old word for a tail. *Rugley* was once thought to have originated in a Clearing where Woodcock were to be found but there is good reason to think that they may have been Snipe. On the other hand *Snipe House* must on no account be taken at its face value. It was originally known as Swinley Snepe, meaning in Old English the Snepe (or Bend in the river) by the Clearing where Swine were kept. This was in 1290. By 1663 the first part of the name had been dropped and only the Snepe remained, until finally it blossomed forth as Snipe House.

This same word Snepe, or Sneape, is reflected in the name of a well known bend in the River Derwent. Yet the names of other farms with apparently the same derivation may well mean nothing of the sort. For instance in the case of *The Sneap* near Bellingham, *The Snape* near Hexham and the Clearing at *Sniperley*, it is the Inhospitable nature of the Land that has most probably provided the explanation.

Ewesley owes its name not to sheep but to Blackbirds, for which the original Clearing must have been notable, and which were known to our forebears as 'osel'—presumably Land-ousels as distinct from Water-ousels.

Rooks and their near relations are, not surprisingly, represented by several names. The *Rookin*, for instance, is just another word for a Rookery. *Crow Hall* was probably in the first place Crow Hill, while *Craster* is the Old Camp, and both *Crawden* and *Crowden Hill* Valleys, where Crows have built. *Ramshope* denotes a Blind Valley inhabited not by sheep but by Ravens.

It might be thought that the derivation of *Cawfields* as the Open Expanse of the Jackdaws was, to say the least of it, unlikely but one has only to visit the place to see the descendants of those same birds of a thousand years ago, circling the neighbouring crags, to appreciate the aptness of the name. *Cawledge Park*, on the other hand, describes the slow-moving Stream where Caua lived, though with *Keyhurst* we return to Jackdaws, this time frequenting a Copse.

Even more confusing is *Pia Troon*, in Allendale, which is something of a curiosity with its Roman and Scottish overtones which are, in fact, pure illusion. The name was originally the Pyot Run, meaning Magpie Walk, and some bonehead, after the two words had been run together, divided them in the wrong place.

It comes as something of a surprise, also, to find several places in

Northumberland that owe their names to the presence of Cranes. Seeing that these birds are virtually unknown in England these days, one might have supposed that what were really involved were Herons. In point of fact, in the Middle Ages at any rate, people seem to have kept pretty quiet about the latter. As Yarrell puts it (in his 'History of British Birds') writing of the palmy days of falconry, 'the places where they bred were almost held sacred; the bird was considered royal game, and penal statutes were enacted for its preservation'. He goes on to say (writing in 1841) 'the Crane was formerly much more frequent ... Sir Thomas Browne of Norwich, who wrote in the time of Charles the Second, says in his works "Cranes are often seen here in hard winters, especially about the champian and fieldy part". Leland ... includes in the bill of fare at the feast of Archbishop Neville, two hundred and four Cranes'.

Cornhill, and *Cornhills* near Kirkwhelpington, remain to remind us of these birds which are still common on the Continent. *Cranecleugh* takes its name from a Ravine where they were to be seen and it is possible that *Cornshields* was a like Shieling, although one must admit that it may have belonged to a man called Corn. A variation is to be found in *Tranwell*—the Stream frequented by Cranes—where the Scandinavian form of the word is used.

If Cranes are no longer with us, Larks (thank goodness) are. Who that has heard it can ever forget the verse in Derwentwater's Lament that runs:

> *No more along the banks of Tyne*
> *I'll rove in autumn grey,*
> *No more I'll hear at early dawn*
> *The Lav'rocks wake the day.*

Lark Hall and *Laverock Hall,* then, are identical and *Laverock Law* closely related.

An altogether more exotic bird is the Loon or Northern Diver, known also as the Ember Goose from the fact that the Norwegians noticed that it appeared on their coast on the Ember days of Advent. Hence also the charming name of Adventsvogel given to it by the

Germans. Why the Hill of *Lumby Law* attracted this bird, however, remains a mystery.

Owls we have already encountered at Outchester, at Ulwham and Ulgham. They have also left their mark on *The Howlett Hall* and on the Marsh of *Owmers*.

It was once thought that *Lucker* was a name of Scandinavian origin derived from their word for a Sandpiper, but it is now fairly certain that the name comes from an Old English word for the Palm or Hollow of one's Hand. *Laker Hall* and *Lickar Moor*, however, probably denote places between two Streams (from 'lacu', meaning not so much a lake as a Stream or Watercourse). On the other hand, *Waughold Holme* really does mean the Water Meadow where the Green Sandpiper plays. This is the bird that Northumbrians call, from the manner in which it flits about like a Waff or puff of wind, a Waffler. Nor is there any reason to suppose that *Wagtail* indicates anything other than appears at first sight.

It might be thought that Hawks were a common form of birdlife when our place names first originated. Without question this was the case but it must be apparent, on reflection, that Clearings, Hills and the like would hardly be named after a bird which is rarely to be seen on tree or ground. So *Hawkwell* is the Spring and *Hauxley*, as well as *Hawkhill*, the Hill where there lived men who were nicknamed Hawk. In an age when sharp sight was of particular importance in the absence of any artificial aids, it is not surprising that a similar nickname was Kite, the Old English word for which was 'glide'. *Gleadscleugh*, therefore, describes the Ravine and *Gleedlee* the Clearing where such a man settled.

Yet if one cannot find a name that owes its origin to Hawks, there is one at least—*Hawkuplea*—that describes the Clearing by the Blind Valley where a Hawker, that is to say a professional flyer of hawks after game, lived.

Last, and for once least, comes the Sparrow. There used to be a house in Cullercoats which bore the crest of the Dove family, who had built it. The neighbours, being firmly under the impression that the bird was a sparrow, always referred to it as Sparrow Hall. Perhaps something of the sort happened to *Sparrow House* near Bothel; or perhaps not. Anyway, the Old English for Sparrow was 'sucga' and hence (most probably) *Sook House* and *Sugley*, the Clearing where Sparrows were to be found.

The possibility of associating any of our place names with Reptiles has been diminished by research. Neither Adderstone nor Etherstone have proved fruitful and even *Paddock Hall* is less likely to be connected with Toads or Frogs than with the Old English 'pearroc', an Enclosure. Only *Paddaburn* may have been called after the Stream where such reptiles were to be found.

Insects, on the other hand, have inspired several names and it will come as no surprise to find that the majority are concerned with Bees. Before the importation of sugar the value of Bees to the community was very considerable. Not only did honey provide virtually the only source of sweetening but beeswax was used in great quantities both in Churches and in the home. When tithes were assessed, therefore, they applied to bees as much as to any farm animals. Even as late as 1840 they are included in the rent charges levied on the parish of Alnham by the Tithe Commissioners, in place of existing tithes that were payable in kind, as follows: —'For every Cow 2d., Calf 4d., Foal 4d., Hive of Bees 4d. Every Householder keeping hens, 6d. as well as a Smoke Pinny of 1d. For every score of ewes milked, 4d.' and so forth.

Equally important was the land from which the nectar was gathered so that a fifteenth-century document concerned with Bavington refers not only to a Guse-croft but also to Honylandes. Earlier still our Anglian forebears had used the word 'gafolheord' to describe a Taxable Herd, or Swarm, of Bees.

Beal, then, is the Bee Hill, *Bickerton* the Beekeeper's Homestead and *Bewick* the Bee Farm. The first Lord of Bewick was one Arkle Moreal (a name sometimes confusingly abbreviated to Merkell) who slew King Malcolm Canmore at the eleventh-century battle of Alnwick and was variously known as 'a most valiant Knight' and as a cowardly assassin, according to which side you happened to be on.

Whereas *Embleton* was settled by a man nicknamed the Caterpillar, and *Emerick* may have been the farm of someone of the same name, *Emblehope* can be regarded as a Blind Valley settled by the Caterpillars themselves. Then *Brizlee* (and probably *Birsley* also) take their names from Hills where Gadflies abound. The first of these bears, apparently, a close resemblance to Mount Carmel. When William de Vesci, Lord of Alnwick, was crusading in Syria, he found at Carmel a Northumbrian Monk, Ralph Fresborn, whom he was allowed to bring back to England on condition that he himself founded a Carmelite monastery: hence Hulne Abbey.

It can hardly have been the same kind of resemblance that prompted someone to give *Mount Carmel* (near Norham) its name, but there is good reason to think that the place was once a kind of staging post for monks from the Border Monasteries journeying to Lindisfarne. Murray's Hall, nearby, and subsequently known as *Morris Hall*, must also have had its attractions. When it was offered for sale in 1870 the advertisement waxed positively lyrical '... wherein 'it ran', a right of salmon and trout rod fishing offers such temptations to the angler whilst into the symphonious ear of the foxhunter the music of the crack packs of the Duke of Buccleuch's and of the Earl of Wemyss' hounds instil vaulting notes of inspiration. Game! as a sequence may be increased indefinitely where, as on the boquet of an estate, the means are so peculiarly adapted towards its propagation'. And again 'The arable and pasture lands throughout are of the most supreme quality, offering a ready solution to the startling problem of the annual increase of rents, with woodlands and fairy dells, gorgeous in the extravagances of Flora's toilette of primroses and wild posies....' Could anyone have resisted buying the place after that? They could; for on this occasion it did not fetch the reserve.

Fleehope, residing as it does at the junction of the College and Flee-hope burns might, one would have thought, owe its name in some way to the meeting of the two waters. Our ancestors, however, called a Fly a 'fleog' and the explanation may well be that it is a Blind Valley where Flies of some sort are unusually troublesome.

Finally there is Brockley Park, now known as *Midgy Ha'*, the 'Hall' infested with Midges. And so a chapter which began with some of the largest of farm animals has finished with one of the smallest (if not the least potent) of insects.

NOTES

[7] cattle.
[8] direction.

CHAPTER 14

I N 1500 the landscape of Northumberland cannot have appeared very different to what it had been a couple of hundred years earlier, and for a very good reason. It was in 1348 that the Black Death struck England. Bad news travels fast and disease travels faster still so that it was not long before Northumberland felt the impact, perhaps not quite so severely as it might if the population had been less scattered, but quite badly enough.

So serious was the decline in population resulting from the Bubonic Plague that where there had been perhaps fifty thousand people in the county a hundred and fifty years previously, the figure had probably risen again to no more than forty thousand by the beginning of the sixteenth century.

There had, in fact, been a complete reversal of fortune in the countryside for, prior to 1348, the population had been rising at such a rate, despite the enormous infant mortality, that there was not enough cleared land to go round. Villages, though most of them would hardly be graced with the name of hamlet today, had become plentiful. A place like Coatyards near Hartburn, for instance, would have taken the form of a whole collection of farms whereas now it is but one. The epidemic, however, had reversed this state of affairs: there was ample cleared land for the survivors and their descendants for several generations to come, so that the land hunger had subsided.

The word 'cot' like so many old words, seems to have had a variety of meanings, or rather shades of meaning which can only have been apparent at the time. In the case of *Coatyards* it would have meant a Sheep Shelter (round which there were Enclosures) and the same idea of a Shelter, or even an Outbuilding, for Animals must have applied not only to such places as Hepscott and Cuddycotes but to *Cote Halls, Cote Hill* and *Cote House* which are all likely to have started life as Dwellings erected where there was already such a Shelter. *Coating Hill* was, in 1547, Cote Hill while *Hemscott Hill* would have been the Hill where Helm Sheltered his stock. *Milescott* is not quite so straightforward: in 1510 it appears as Perton Myles Cotes but, in 1547, as Midlescoote, which must have been the Middle Building. The Cotes in this case were presumably human habitations in the form of rude shelters. *Cottingwood*, however, has a totally different derivation and signifies the Wood of Cotta's People.

At this time there would not have been a great number of farms in Northumberland in the modern sense of the word: that is to say, more or less isolated and self supporting tracts of arable and grass land. Yet there must have been more in this county than further south where conditions were perhaps more favourable to people huddling together in the modern fashion. In fact a 'farm' or 'tenement' tended to be a mechanical subdivision of the manor, each amounting to roughly thirty acres. These acres were spread over the 'town fields' and the farmer's house would be one of a collection of buildings making up the 'town'. As well as the Toft and the Croft or Allotment, such as Hicca's at *Hitchcroft*, there might be a Garth; a word that has evolved from the Old English 'geard' and meant an Enclosure that was private to the occupier. 'Geard' has since become the modern Yard.

Yardhope, for instance, signifies a Blind Valley where there was such an Enclosure, that is to say a small patch of ground individually tilled. Such an Enclosure on a Hill has inspired two names as different from each other as *Earle* (the pronounciation of which betrays its origin as Yard-Hill) and *Guards Hill*. The name, *Earsdon*, of course is pronounced quite differently and denotes, in both instances where it appears, the Hill of Eanred or Eored. A reminder of the enclosures that went with the Manor House of the De Lisles of Woodburn is to be found in *Hallyards*.

The hamlets which dotted the countryside were still known as 'towns', a word which had originated in the Old English 'tun', or Homestead, and that appears not only in the Family Homesteads, previously discussed, but in (for instance) *Lanton*, the Long Homestead. Or of course the name of the original settler might be invoked, such as Gunnwara at *Gunnerton*, Paelloc at *Paston*, Cynemaer at *Kimmerston*, or Ulfi at *Ouston* (as also at the Clearing of *Oustley*).

The derivation of *Wooperton*, however is more involved. The oldest known form of the name is Wepredane or Wepreden and is thought to signify the Valley by the Hill with a Temple on it: it has therefore nothing to do with a Homestead at all.

Each 'town was more or less self sufficient. Not only would it have its own Bakery and the use (in exchange for a 'multure' or payment in corn) of the Lord's Mill, but its own Tannery. Spinning, weaving and the making of clothes took place in the home and timber was to be had for specific purposes. The right of 'turbary', which the villagers also enjoyed, entitled them to cut Turf from the common pit with which to roof their houses. The local term for a Turf is a Divot: hence *Divot Hill* near Bavington. The word Turf was used to describe the undisturbed Sward so that *Turf House* is the Dwelling, and *Turve Laws* the Hill(s), where the Grass is particularly good.

Round the hamlet, or township, would be three or four Town Fields sown with Barley, Beans or Wheat and fallowed in rotation. Each field was divided into Furlongs, that is to say, pieces of land about a furrow long; a furrow in turn being as far as you could get a team of oxen to plough without giving them a breather, or about two hundred and twenty yards.

In Northumberland these divisions were called not Furlongs but Shots, from the Old English 'sceat'. This word seems, as usual, to have had many different shades of meaning in that the piece of land which it denoted might be soil that was left untilled, or overgrown with trees, or precisely the reverse, so that it could signify a ride or glade in the forest. In fact it seems to have described pretty well any piece of land that looked different from its surroundings. *Buckshott*, then, had nothing to do with the shooting of buck but took its name from a Strip of ground on which Goats were kept.

The original meaning of Cockshott would be the Glade in a wood where Woodcock are to be found. The next development was the 'granting of a Cockshott' which entitled the recipient to spread nets for Woodcock for one year in a specified glade. Finally a 'cockshut' came to mean the net itself and, as this was always rigged at twilight, we find Shakespeare and his contemporaries alluding to the darkening as 'cockshut time'. *Cockshott* then is the Glade where such a Net was set up.

Landshott owes its derivation to another technical term, derived from the same root but denoting land for which an Allotted Price has been paid; perhaps the equivalent of the Scandinavian 'Kaupland' or Bought Land which gave *Coupland* and (possibly) *Little Coop House* their name.

The Shots in the Town fields normally ran parallel to each other but the contour of the ground or other factors could cause one group of them to run at right angles to the rest and to be separated from them by a Headrig. In each Shot were a number of strips, each worked by a different farmer and divided from the next by a Balk or Ridge of unploughed land, so *Howbalk* means the Hollow where the Land was Unploughed, or there was a Terrace, while *High Balks* denoted the same but on Higher Land.

If the Town Field was shaped so that these cultivated strips tapered like a wedge, they were known as Gores (as in Overgrass) but if they were cut short by abutting on some obstacle they were known as Butts, and indeed the short furrows in an awkwardly shaped field are so described to this day. In the same way *Muckley Butts* describes a place that Abuts on two townships and takes its name from a Big Clearing, just as *Muckleridge* denotes a Big Ridge.

Each farmer was granted, in addition to his arable strips, the use in rotation of a proportion of the Town Leazes or Common Meadow from which he could cut hay. The field was thrown open, once the hay had been carried, to all the villagers, on which to pasture their stock. These Meadows are perpetuated in such names as *Leazes House* and *Lees Farm* and also in *Snableazes* where the grass lay near a Projecting Rock or Rocky part of the Hill.

Then there was the Waste that was Common to all and might consist either of Rough Grazing or of Woodland or of both. This was normally 'stinted': that is to say each villager was allowed to pasture on it a specified number of animals. He also enjoyed certain rights which have already been discussed, which might also be stinted in the sense of being restricted to so much timber, so much turf and so forth. Alternatively they might be enjoyed 'without stint', an expression which is, of course, still in use, though without any general realisation of what it implies.

In return for the land which he held, each farmer would be expected to provide the Lord of the Manor annually with so many days of work on the Demesne, or Home Farm. For instance, at Mul's Fen or Marsh (now known as *Mousen*, but originally called after someone who was a 'mule' or half-breed) 'Hyde Mulessen' farmed, in the reign of Henry III, part of the demesne land of Bamburgh Castle on the following conditions. He had to plough for one day a year on the main farm with six ploughs at the bailiff's pleasure, being provided on that day with one meal (it is to be hoped for each ploughman) at the King's expense. He had to carry corn for one day each autumn with twelve wagons, being provided once more with a meal, and to 'reap in autumn' for three days with twelve men on the same terms.

Indeed as lately as 1784, we find that when certain land changed hands, satisfaction had to be made for 'all yearly rents or annual payments, heriots, mow dargues and shear dargues or day works, hens and catches or carriages to the town of Hexham'.

A Heriot takes its name from the Old English 'here', signifying an Army, and another word denoting Equipment, for it was originally the Lord's right to be supplied with the trappings of war and, in particular, a horse. From this beginning it turned into the right of the Lord of the Manor to the best beast (or chattel) on the farm when the tenant died. There was indeed a classic case at law in the nineteenth century when the Lord of a Manor in Essex tried to exercise his right by claiming a racehorse worth thousands of pounds, and failed. In any case the tenant (or rather his executors) should, by law, have been allowed to opt out by paying the significant sum of forty shillings.

A Dargue was the technical term for a day's work owed to the Lord of the Manor and was called a Boon Dargue if it were provided at what we should now call a peak period. It might be required at harvest-time, as in the case of Hyde Mulessen; at clipping time or at whatever time was laid down in the agreement under which the tenant held his land. In the end the word also came to mean the amount of land that could be ploughed in a day and therefore, in this special sense, an Acre. Thus the equivalent of Bob Acres in 'The Rivals' could be Bob Dargues and, indeed, the surname is not uncommon today, at any rate in the North of England. Sometime in the sixteenth century the farm of Smallburn, in Redesdale, was divided between the families of Dargue and Dunn: hence the origin of *Dargues*, *Dargues Hope* (or Blind Valley) and *Dunn's Houses*.

If the year 1500 showed no increase in the population of Northumberland and little change in the system under which people lived and farmed, neither would there have been any perceptible improvement in their roads.

In medieval times, and until the advent of the Turnpike there were a number of different kinds of 'road', each one worse than the last. First came the Highway which was usable at drier times of the year, but at no other, for wains—that is to say wagons—so that we get a name like *Wainford Rigg*, the Ridge near the Ford that could be used by Wagons, and *Carterway Heads*, the Hill traversed by a Road usable by Carts: perhaps also *Wainhope*, the Blind Valley that Wagons could traverse. Such a road naturally followed the harder ground and lighter soils, a necessity that led to twists and turns that might otherwise be inexplicable. If it proved absolutely necessary to cross marsh, or even clay land, the road might be built up on a Causeway, producing names like *Corse Hall* (still known in 1769 as Causeway Houses) and *Causey Park*. It is perhaps worth mentioning that the derivation of *Corsenside* is quite different, for this was the Hill Pasture belonging to Crossan.

Secondly, there were the old Paved Roads, either left by the Romans or 'made-up' with stone. These were known as Streets and gave their name to *Street House* near Ponteland and to the Street-tun (or Homestead) that became *Sturton Grange*. *Stannington* was originally Stan-weg-tun, the Homestead by the Stone (or Paved) Way while *Clattering Houses*, near Ellingham, took its name from the Sound that horses' hooves made on a Paved Road. That this name was in no way abnormal is borne out by a reference in 1580 to 'the street called the Clatterandway', near Whittingham. In 1702 the same road was known as the Clattering Causeway.

The trade in Salt used to be of the greatest importance in Northumberland, as everywhere else in the world. It has already been pointed out that each 'town' was very largely self-supporting, but this was one absolutely essential item of diet that could not be produced at home but had to be 'imported'. This made Salt an attractive subject for taxation by the Crown and complaints were fairly constant that the inflated price limited the amount that was sold. The traffic itself was so considerable that there came into being special Salt Roads, so that we find that 'the antient paved road or saltway led to the Duddens and Saltwick and the western parts of the county and from Hartford Bridge wants improving'.

The Duddens, now known as *North* and *South Duddo*, took their name from Dudda's Valley, unlike *Duddo* near Norham which was the Spur of a Hill where another Dudda lived. *Saltwick*, with its traditional connection with the Salters' Bridge and Salters' Road in Gosforth, was the 'wic where salt was sold'. In other words the Farm was used as what we would now call a wholesale outlet for the salt manufactured at *Hartley Pans*, at *Cowpen* and elsewhere. The latter, indeed, took its name not from any enclosure for cows but from the Old English 'cupum', meaning At the Cups or Pans (where Salt was evaporated). It was a valuable source of income to the Monks of Brinkburn Priory to whom it belonged.

Another Salt Road followed the line of a prehistoric track from the mouth of the Tyne into Scotland through *Alnham*. This is the Village on the river known to Ptolemy in the year 150 as Alaunos. Alnham was also the subject of an impassioned protest by the Earl of Northumberland to Henry VIII that the Scots had 'brunte a town of mine called Alnham, with all the corne, hay and householde stuf in the said town'; then, rather as an afterthought, 'also a woman'. The same river, of course, lends its name to the Farm of *Alnwick*, the Earthwork of *Alndyke* and to *Alnmouth*. The latter competes with *Whittingham* (the village of Hwita's People) for the distinction of being the Twyford (or place of Two Fords) where, according to the Venerable Bede, the great Synod was held at which Cuthbert was chosen to be Bishop of Lindisfarne. Expert opinion now awards the verdict to Alnmouth.

Despite a certain amount of 'paving', these Salt Roads must have ranked among the lesser roads which were passable only by the trains of packhorses that at certain times of the year, and in most parts of the county, were the only conceivable method of moving goods from one place to another.

Further down the scale again were the Drift or Drove Roads, the ancient paths trodden by cattle, sheep and geese which, avoiding all highways and centres of population, wound their way in some cases the whole distance from Scotland to London. Some of the herds of cattle being driven south to Barnet Fair would have been more than two miles long. Occasionally they had the benefit of minor bridges such as that which gave its name to *The Brig* near Woodburn, but normally they would ford each river as they came to it, crossing the Tyne, for instance, just west of Newburn.

It has been calculated that thirty thousand cattle were driven down from Scotland alone every year, a great number of which passed through Northumberland. They would take seven to eight weeks on the road and would be shod at least once to enable them to complete the journey. Yet, with the exception of *Kypie*, which must have been on a Cow-path, these roads do not seem to have left any impression on our place names. There are, however, certain fields whose names commemorate the lairages (that is to say the enclosures into which the animals in question could be driven at night) which were such an essential part of the system.

Then there were the Lanes which were principally of local value and known sometimes in Northumberland as Chares, a name recognisable at the present day mainly in the narrower streets of our towns. Thus Lord Chancellor Eldon was 'born in a Chair-foot' in Newcastle. Names of hills like King's Chair and Shepherd's Chair refer to rock formations in the form of a Seat but *Chair Heads*, near Whitfield, marks the Hill up which a Lane goes as does *Chair Head* near Corbridge. The Lane might, of course, be a Winding one such as gave *Wynding House* its name, or a Loaning, Loan or Lonnen.

There was also a specialised meaning attached to a Grass Lane near the village, for in this case it might represent the place where Cows or Ewes were milked, as witness that verse of The Flowers of the Forest commemorating the Battle of Flodden : —

I've heard them lilting, at our ewe milking,
Lasses a'lilting, before dawn of day:
But now they are moaning on ilka green loaning;
The flowers o' the forest are a' wede away.

After hundreds of years it is impossible to ascribe the precise meaning to *Loaning House, Loaning End* and *Loaning Side.* Suffice it to say that, like *Loansdean* where there is a Valley, and *Foul Loaning*, which no doubt was muddy, they are concerned with a Lane, or Lonnen, of some kind.

The practice of milking ewes as well as cows persisted for long enough, time consuming as it must have been, and it was sufficiently important to inspire a word 'bucht', meaning the byre or shelter where the milking was done in winter. There are a great number of fields called Bowt Hill, or something of that sort, and there are two farms as well, of which *Bought Hill* in North Tynedale bears this meaning certainly, and Longboat very probably.

Finally, of course, there were the Tracks or Paths such as the 'peth' beside which Hod lived—now known as *Hudspeth*—or the continuation of Dere Street called *Gamelspath,* which led northwards to the Roman staging post at Chew Green. Close by is *Mackendon* or Macca's Hill. It is a curious fact that whenever there was an old established road that could be explained in no other way, our ancestors ascribed it without hesitation to the activities of Satan (or the Old One) as in Gamelspath; another obvious instance being the Devil's Causeway.

Near Blanchland is a place called *Gingleshaugh* which has been explained as the Low-lying Ground by the Green Clearing. In 1663, however, there appears a place 'near Shotley' described as 'Ginglehaugh or Gamillshaugh' and it appears at least as likely that this was The Old Man's Haugh, if not the devil's own. Yet *Gingle Pot* takes its name from the Echoing Pool in the River Allen.

Where there were roads, there were necessarily Fords, for bridges were rare indeed up to the thirteenth century and, thereafter, few and far between. Sometimes they would be named after the person who lived beside them, such as *Doxford* after Docc and *Allensford* after Aleyn (whose namesake lived at *Allens Green). Usway Ford* is called after Osa, a name which may well have been a corruption of Oswy, the Seventh Christian King of Northumbria.

Usually, however, the name described the physical circumstances. *Ford* itself hardly needs explaining while *Stamford, Stakeford* and *Styford* denote Fords that were Stony or Marked by a Stake, or associated with a Path. *Annitsford* goes one better because it was probably connected with a Steep Path. *Gosforth* is almost invariably explained as the Goose Ford, which really does not make much sense when one considers the amphibious nature of these creatures. The stream, originally called the Yese, was subsequently known as the Ouse or Goose Burn and there seems little doubt that Gosforth denotes the Goose Burn Ford. *Holford* is the Hollow, or Deep, Ford and *Mitford* the Ford at the Junction (of the Wansbeck and the Font) and *not* the Middle Ford.

At *Langleeford*, by the Long Clearing, Sir Walter Scott and his uncle used to go and stay in the farmhouse. It was of this place that he wrote 'So much simplicity resides among these hills that a pen, which could write at least, was not to be found about the house, though belonging to a considerable farmer, till I shot the crow with whose quill I write this epistle'.

Whether or not the original Twyford was Whittingham, mention of the latter provides a reminder that there remain many names of the same type in the county that we have not discussed since Ovingham. All, with the exception of *Chillingham*, which we shall deal with later, are pronounced with a soft 'g' and all have the meaning of the Village of the People of So-and-So or from somewhere-or-other. *Ealingham*, for example, was founded by Eofel, *Edlingham* by Eadwulf, *Eglingham* by Eegwulf and *Ellingham* by Ella (perhaps the same person whose name is perpetuated by Elwick). In the case of *Risingham* the original Hrisa must have had a flying start for the place began life as the Roman station of Habitancum. It was supposed to be defended by the god Mogon, since when it was traditionally known as the Town of the Giants. This may explain the curious figure cut in the rock, that is known as Robin of Risingham but which bears a certain resemblance to a Roman centurion.

Beltingham is less easy to derive. If, like Bellingham, it is the village of the people who lived on the hill, how has the 't' crept in? Another possibility is that it is the Village of Boltr's People in which case, as in that of Boltshope, the founder would have been a Scandinavian.

CHAPTER 15

Eslington for bonny lasses, Callaly for craws,
Whittingham for white bread, Thrunton for faws.

So runs another of those pointless jingles of which our ancestors, when crowing on their particular dunghill, seem to have been so fond. *Eslington* means the Homestead of Aescel's people: Callaly, Whittingham and even breadmaking in general we have already considered, but *Thrunton* (Thurwine's Homestead) is worth looking at in more detail. On Thrunton Moor there lived one Jamie McFarlane who made Besoms for his daughter Meg to hawk around the district, going as far afield as Glendale to *Fishestead*, a Steading or Farm which probably owes its name to the Curing, rather than the catching of Fish. Anyone who havered or wavered was in danger of being told 'Ye're like Meg McFarlane who had twenty hundred minds whether to go for the night to Whittingham or Fishestead. *The Besom Farm* at Longframlington presumably owes its name to one of Jamie's competitors.

But Thrunton, according to rhyme, was also famous for 'faws', or Faas as they are more commonly known; in other words the Gipsy tribe that had their headquarters for hundreds of years at Yetholm, just over the Border. So powerful were they that in 1540 James V of Scotland was moved to require all sheriffs to 'assist John Fall, Lord and Erle of Little Egypt, in executing justice upon his company and folkis, conforming to the Laws of Egypt and in punissing of all them that rebellis against him'. *Old Egypt*, then, which is just on the Northumbrian side of the Border needs little explanation.

Nearby lies *Tiptoe*. People called De Tipetot keep cropping up during the thirteenth and fourteenth centuries. In 1281 Robert of that ilk bore witness to a charter granting the right to hold a market at York and in 1345 John de Clavering, Baron of Warkworth, married the daughter of another Robert Tipetot. Now there is no such place in Normandy, so it seems almost certain that the name is a frenchification of what we now call Tiptoe. In 1860 the spelling seems to have been Tipthoe and this is entirely in accordance with the actual situation of the farm which seems to stick out over the Till. It must have started life, in fact, as Aet-yppe-hoh, that is to say At the Plateau on the Spur of the Hill.

Another name with a somewhat similar derivation is *Tipalt*, which was originally Aet-yppe-wold, At the Plateau with a Wood, and a third of the same kind may be that mysterious place *Tuperee*, At the Plateau by the Water.

James' instructions to his sheriffs (or shire-reeves) is a reminder of the effect which that important figure, the Reeve, has had on the place names of Northumberland.

A Reeve, or Grieve as he was known in Scotland and in parts of Northumberland, was elected by the farmers of the township as being its best husbandman. It was his duty to supervise the working of the town fields that were common to all and to ensure that everyone got a fair deal. He was supervised in turn by the Bailiff of the Lord of the Manor who, of course, had a vested interest in the way in which the manor was farmed.

The Bailiff not only ensured that his master enjoyed the rights that were his, but was charged particularly with seeing that the demesne land was properly looked after. To this end he employed a Hayward whose job it was to keep an eye on the Woods, on the Corn and Meadow Land and on the harvesting of Corn and Hay—in fact he must have been the general foreman or steward of the home farm. The Bailiff would also employ a Ploughman, Waggoner, Cowherd, Swineherd, Shepherd and Dairymaid.

The terms Reeve and Bailiff seem to have been to some extent interchangeable. For instance as lately as this century there were to be found not only the Noltherds of Newcastle, who looked after the Freemen's cattle, but the Herd and Moor Grieves of Alnwick. In point of fact, the word Reeve simply denotes responsibility on behalf of another, or of others. In Chaucer's 'Reeve's tale', therefore, he is the Lord's Bailiff or Agent.

> *Well couthe he keep a garner and a bin,*
> *There was non auditor couth on him winn.*
> *Well wist he by the drought and by the raine*
> *And yelding of his sede and of his graine.*
> *His Lordis shepe, his nete[9] and his deirie,*
> *His swine, his hors, his store and his pultrie,*
> *Were wholly in this Reeve' is governing;*
> *And by his covenaunt gave he reckening.*

Grievestead takes its name from the Farm where a Reeve lived, and so does *Greysteads* near Bellingham, which was known in the seventeenth century as Grievesteads, while *Greaves Ash* (once Greaves Folc Ash) reminds us of the Ash Tree near where such a person or his dependents, lived. The same rendering of the word appears not only at Alnwick but in the parish of Allendale which used to be divided into six grieveships.

The other rendering is to be found in *Reaveley Mires*, the Marsh near the Reeve's Clearing, and (rather surprisingly) in *Rivergreen* near Mitford, which was known in 1277 as Revehow—the Spur of a Hill farmed by the Reeve. Even *Reaver Hill*, sad to say, probably has none of the romantic associations with Mosstroopers that one might expect, but also denotes a Reeve's dwelling, while *Riffington* may well have been the Homestead of the Reeve's People.

Among the Barons (as distinct from the Lords of the Manor) it seems to have been the height of ambition to be granted not only the Right of Infangthief and Outfangthief but of Gallows as well. In other words, they wanted the power to arrest anyone in their own service who had done wrong, and also those in the service of others who were unwise enough to stray into their barony: then, if the fancy took them, to hang the malefactors on their private gallows.

So *Gallowhill* was where the Barons of Bolam executed the malefactors that they 'fanged' (in other words, caught), *Gallow shaw* the Copse near a Gallows, and *Gallowshield Rigg* the Ridge where a

Summer Hut was so delightfully situated.

Then there is *Gallowshill*, near Hartington, where the Barons of Bolbec did their hanging, and where once the giant Reay brothers lived. One of these, being unwise enough to attack a posse of Scottish Mosstroopers single-handed, was 'cut into collops' and taken home in a sheet. The name of *Bolam*, meaning At the Boles, or Tree Trunks, is significant because it brings home to us the necessity which led our ancestors laboriously to hack down great quantities of trees in order to clear their land for cultivation, and to make a pile of the resultant timber. *Hartington* originates from the Homestead by the Stags' Path.

Another Gallows was operated by the Barons of *Bothal*, a place which takes its name from the Low Ground by the river where Bota happened to settle. These were at *Stobhill*, so called because of the Stobs or Tree stumps that covered the Hill, as in the case of *Stobby Lea* and of *Stobswood*.

It was at *Low Stublick* (the Enclosure where there were Tree stumps) that on July 7th 1852 in a violent thunderstorm 'the electric fluid entered a dwelling house occupied by Thomas Stokoe, killing a dog lying underneath a chair which Mr Stokoe was sitting upon: it also turned an eight-day clock completely round, taking a large piece off the case: and dashed a female against a door, smashing it open.... At Nubbock farm about one mile and a half from Low Stublick there was scarcely a drop of rain. They were occupied clipping sheep all that day and were never once stopped by the rain'. Lucky Mr Stokoe!

Just as there are more ways of killing a cat than stuffing it with cream, so there are (or were) more ways of getting rid of undesirable members of the community than by hanging. *Wreigh Hill* in Coquetdale, for instance, was the Felons' Hill where those who offended against society were quietly strangled. It was also the birthplace of Coughran the infant prodigy, whose mathematical genius was such that he finished up as Calculator to the Astronomer Royal—a kind of human computer.

The Scots once devastated the place (in 1412) so thoroughly that the 'woeful Wednesday of the Wreck Hill' not only became a by-word but caused some to think that it was the wrecking from which the name was derived. In fact it comes from the Old English 'wearg' (a felon) and thereby hangs a tale. Near Throckley runs the Wreigh burn (pronounced Reeth) where yet another method of disposing of malefactors was practised, this time by drowning. Not far away is a building estate where the street nearest to the burn is named after it (more or less) Reeth Way. One wonders if the residents are aware of the full enormity of a situation that has caused them to live on the Felons' Way.

Perhaps this is as good a place as any to discuss a kind of crime (if that is the right word) associated with some of our villages and farms even if it has not, in most cases, affected their names. This is smuggling, and its headquarters were at *Boulmer*. Called after one Bulla who used to live by the Mere (in this case a Sea-pool) the place gave its name to Boulmer Gin, a euphemism that denoted the smuggled variety.

The actual distribution of the spirit was a highly organised operation which took place, of course, at night and must have been winked at more often than not; otherwise it could not have survived as long as it did. At *Bushygap*, for instance—a place whose name is thought to mean exactly what it says—that is to say a Bush or Thicket in a Gap in the Moors, a double gable in the farmhouse was constructed especially for the purpose of storing the liquor.

> And Bob Dunn o' the Forest
> He's riding te Boomer for gin,
> Wi' three famed horses fra' Bushy Gap Lonnen
> But 'Kate o' the West' is the Queen o' them aa.

The Forest, of course, was what is still known as Rothbury Forest and, like Coquetdale, was by no means dependent on foreign spirits. The whole district seems to have been thick with illicit stills owned by men who thought with Robbie Burns that 'Freedom and Whisky gang thegether'. It may have been another of these stills, if it was not a depot for the distribution of what they produced, that gave to *Whisky Cleugh*, near Humbleton, its name.

The stills were generally hacked out of the rock but no doubt there could have been used one of the vast cauldrons of the period such as gave *Chattlehope* its name of the Valley whose end is shaped like a Kettle.

It must, indeed, have been tempting to liken the shape of a valley or hill to some well-known object for there are many such names to be found. *Spithope Hall*, describing another Valley whose end is shaped like a Spit, is another and *Codlaw Dene*, the Valley by the Hill shaped like a Bag, is a third. *Nesbitt*, near Stamfordham and *Nesbit*, near Doddington, were both known in 1242 as Nesebit or Nesebite which is identical with the North country word for 'the iron that passes across the nose of a horse'. In each case however there is a Nose-shaped Hill involved so there is little doubt that the proper derivation is the Nose-shaped Bight, or Bend, of a Hill.

A further name for a Point of Land is to be found in *Ord* and in *Ordley*, the Clearing shaped like the Point of a Sword. Yet another appears in *The Steel*, and in *Steel* which is the Point of Land between the Rowley Burn and the Devils Water; in all probability the very place described as Dennisburn where King Cadwallon was finally overtaken and killed after the battle of Heavenfield. *Steelrigg* has a somewhat different meaning, denoting a Ridge with a Steep Path.

Then there is *Snook Bank* which also denotes a Sharp Point. In 1264 it was known by a name of truly Teutonic complexity—Schakelzerdesnoke, meaning the Schackleyard (or place where cows were tied by the neck) near such a Point. At *Rock* (the place by the Rock[s]) is *Rock Nab*, and this again denotes a Nose or Point while *Howick Scar* describes a Bare, or Broken, Rock near the High Farm.

When Edward I was described as Long Shanks or, later on, one talked about 'travelling by Shanks' Pony' the allusion, of course, was to Legs and it is the same word which also appears in such places as *Shankfoot* and *Shankhead*, the Bottom and Top of Points of a Hill that project like a shinbone, and in *Letham Shank* where there was a Village on a Slope. Yet at *Shankhouse* there is no such hill so that the name in this case must refer to a Cup-shaped Depression.

In many cases the surface rather than the shape of the hill has inspired the name of a place. *The Scaup*, for instance, just denotes a Rugged, Steep place. Another such name, deceptive enough in all conscience, is *Crops Hall* which has nothing to do with crops as we known them but everything to do with Outcrops of rock. It is quite

possible that the most Knobbly of all is *Hobberlaw*, near Alnwick.
In 1296 it was known as Bertewell, the Bright Spring. By 1569, however, so many excrescences had appeared on it in the shape of
quarries, and even a limekiln, that it appears as 'Byrtwell or Uberlow'
and finally Hobberlaw, the Hill covered with Hummocks.

Another name that may be connected with the shape or surface of
the hill is *Peighills*, shown on Armstrong's map of 1769 as Pig Hills.
It seems more likely, however, that the place is named after Peohtea.
The desire to associate a hill with pigs appears again in *Ogle*, known
at one time as Hoghill. In fact the Hill here was called after Ocga, the
son of King Ida.

Or the Hill may be broken by quarrying. It is possible that *Penny
Hill* and *Penny Laws*, for example, originally provided the Penny
Stanes that were used in olden days for quoits. Near Blanchland,
however, there is a farm named, somewhat similarly, *Penny Pye*, for
which there is a quite different explanation. There used to be a
custom in Northumberland of paying someone like the Blacksmith
for the different parts of a job as they were completed, instead of
waiting till the end (or longer). This was known as Penny Pay and it
does not seem unreasonable to suppose that some previous occupier
of the farm was an exponent of this admirable practice, particularly
as a drove road passed nearby and there is evidence that shoes were
made there with which to protect the feet of the cattle on their long
journey from Scotland to East Anglia and elsewhere. The alternative
to Penny Pay must have been a good deal less attractive to the Blacksmith: at one time, for instance, he used to receive 'Sharping Corn'
and 'Laying Corn' for sharpening and laying farming tools. This
was payable at harvest and until then, presumably, he had to whistle
for his money.

NOTE

[9] cattle.

CHAPTER 16

God send the land deliv'rance
Frae every reiving, riding Scot:
We'll sune hae neither cow nor ewe;
We'll sune hae neither stag nor stot.

IN the interval between 1500, when we last took a birdseye look at Northumberland, and the end of that century, a good deal of progress should have been evident, at least in the more peaceable parts of the county. Here, as in the rest of England, it must have appeared as 'a green and quiet agricultural country in which miles of deep forest alternated with 1000-acre "fields" of barley, beans or wheat, or with variegated heaths and bleak moors, and little pasture closes'.

On the other hand those districts that were readily accessible to the Scots would have been anything but quietly agricultural, for this was the heyday of the Mosstroopers—'honest men, save doing a little shifting for their living' in order to alleviate the monotony of rearing cattle and sheep. Following the Battle of Flodden there were no major wars between Scots and English, and a kind of uneasy peace, broken only by an infinite number of minor conflagrations, was achieved instead.

It cannot have made very much difference to the inhabitants of the valleys of North Tyne, Rede and Coquet whether an official war was in progress or not for they, like their Scottish neighbours, had still to live in a permanent state of defence. A typical 'town', then, consisted of a few mud and timber hovels huddled round what had become its focal point—the Peel Tower—into which animals could be driven directly the alarm was given and in whose upper stories human beings might also shelter. It has even been suggested that this explains the name *Shidlaw*, the Hill where cattle and sheep were Shed to their rightful owners after being driven into Wark Castle to preserve them from the Scots.

Only rarely, however, have these Peels, which were such a notable feature of the countryside and whose remains are still evident all over Northumberland, been commemorated in the names of places. Certainly *Staward Peel* describes such a Tower by a Stony Enclosure and *Peel Well* (near Bardon Mill) the Spring by a Tower. In the latter case, however, it is one of the Turrets of the Roman Wall, and not a fortification built for the purpose, that is perpetuated in the name.

The Peels, near Alwinton, shows no traces of a tower of any kind and the explanation seems to be that this was originally part of the demesne land belonging to Harbottle Castle which happened to be fenced round with Pales. *Peel Flatt*, near Slaley, has a different derivation again for the name refers to a piece of Flat ground that is Bare. It echoes, in fact, that verse of Ezekiel which declares that 'every head was made bald and every shoulder peeled'.

Very often the raiders, when they arrived, would pick up any outlying cattle or sheep and make off without further ado, though hotly pursued by the owners. There was, indeed, a code of conduct laid down for these occasions, that appeared in the Border Laws administered by the Wardens of the Marches whose business it had become to keep the peace between the two countries. The normal response was the Hot Trod in which 'pursuit with hue and cry, with horse and hound' was actually compulsory, so that everyone was enjoined to assist and anybody who impeded the chase was liable to punishment. But there was also the Cold Trod, which was not encouraged but permitted subject to certain conditions. The injured party was to be given safe conduct in the offender's country for six days, and in beginning the Cold Trod he must 'go unto some honest man inhabiting within the Marches which he hath entered and declare unto him the cause of his entry'. In this particular locality it must have been about as difficult to find the honest man as to run to earth the stock that had been lifted.

Occasionally the raiders (and anything that applies to the Scots must have been equally applicable to the Northumbrians) would not be content with rounding up the cattle and leaving. There exists a very descriptive poem by Crawhall that begins: —

> *Wae's me—God wot—but the Beggarlie Scot*
> *Through the 'bateable lands has prickit his waie*

It then goes on to describe the natural response of the Scottish Moss-troopers to the retirement of the locals into their Peel tower: —

> *For they scumfish*[10] *them oot wi' the smoutherin straw.*

The whole business of keeping watch and ward was also organised by the Wardens of the Marches and it was strictly laid down how many men should be forthcoming, on pain of punishment, from each 'ward' and at what fords or passes they should be posted. It is not surprising, therefore, to find a number of farms dotting the countryside with names like *Watch Hill, Spy Law, Look-Out, Keek-out, View Law* and *Viewley*, the last two having exactly the same meaning.

Tuthill is also the Watch Hill, while *Warton* is the Homestead where Ward was kept and the same Old English 'weard' is found in *Warden*, the Ward Hill, and therefore in *Warden Battocks*, a name that refers to the Low Ground by the River. *Watch Law* enters history as the Hill from which the Earl of Surrey kept an eye on the Scots as they advanced to Branxton to begin the battle of Flodden.

Other places where a watch must have been kept are *Glantlees*, the Look-out Clearing and *Glanton*, the Look-out Hill. Glanton, later on, seems to have been quite a military centre. Here, for instance, were the headquarters of that fine body of men, the Royal Cheviot Legion Cavalry, which was one of the many volunteer forces that were raised in order to repel the invasion threatened by Napoleon. It may well have been at this time that *Beacon Rigg* and *The Beacon Farm* earned their names. At any rate it was in 1804 that a beacon was ignited by mistake and the Cheviot Legion actually stood to arms, and marched to the coast under the command of that flamboyant character, Count Horace St Paul of Ewart.

In 1806 we find many of the same names appearing in the ranks of the Coquetdale Rangers of Volunteer Cavalry, two members of which, according to Dippie Dixon, lived for many years afterwards at Whittingham where they earned scant respect. Trooper Vint's only experience of being under fire appears to have been when he accidentally shot himself in the leg with his own carbine. According to Dippie Dixon, the village children used to make a practice of taunting the poor old man by singing: —

> *Reed-backed bummeller,*
> *Cock-tailed tummeller,*
> *Fire-side soldier,*
> *Darna' gan te war.*

Wisp Law, in all probability, derives its names from being a Hill where the Wisp, or Lighted bunch of Straw on the end of a spear, was raised. This was the traditional signal to gather for a raid against the old enemy, among whom, incidentally, the Hot Trod itself was often known as 'the brennin strae'. That the initiative did not always lie with the Scots is apparent when Shakespeare makes Henry IV refer to Harry Hotspur as 'he that kills me some six or seven dozen of Scots at a breakfast, washes his hands, and says to his wife, "Fie upon this quiet life! I want work" '.

It was, for instance, one of the most important of the Border Laws that every ward should be assessed on its ability to provide men 'able in horse and harness' who could be relied upon in case of invasion, small or great. Thus in 1584 the old tower at the Homestead by the Cold Lakes known as *Coldmartin* was described as 'one towre of stane and Lime of Roger Fowberry's of Fowberry, Gent, Utterly Decayed notwithstanding it hath land belonging to it able to keep 2 men and horse fit for service'. It must have been this place that subsequently gave *Tower Martin* its name.

Nevertheless it was a Scotsman in the shape of an early Walter Scott, known more familiarly as Wat o'Harden who, when returning through Northumberland with a 'bow[11] of Kye and a bassen'd[12] bull', set eyes on a haystack and exclaimed 'By my soul, had ye but four feet, ye should not stand lang there'.

And perhaps the last word (or rather words, for there are many) should be allowed to another Scot in the shape of the Bishop of Glasgow, who cursed those on his own side of the border that 'all the malesouns and waresouns that ever gat warldlie creatur sen the beginning of the warld to this hour mot licht apon yaim. I curse thair heid, and all ye haris of thair heid; I curse thair face, thair een, thair mouth, thair neise, thair towng. thair teith; thair craig, thair schulders, thair breist, thair hert; thair stomck, thair bak, thair wame, thair armes, thair leggis, thair handes, thair feit and everilk part of thair body, fra the top of thair heid to the soill of thair feit, before and behind, within and withoute'.

It may seem curious, after all this, to find that, even at the height of the unofficial border warfare, great numbers of Scots were settled and living happily in Northumberland, as is still (one hopes) the case. According to Cadwallader Bates, writing about this, the six-teenth century, 'the immense number of Scots settled in Northum-berland had long been a source of complaint. In Moneylaws (near Carham) there was not an Englishman left. Generally speaking every third man along the Border was a Scot in the service of a Northum-brian master'.

Lest it be thought that the name *Moneylaws* may have provided some special attraction it should be pointed out that the name only denotes Many Hills, while *Sunilaws*, not so far away, probably de-scribes the Hill(s) where Sunni lived. *Carham* simply means At the Rocks.

Nevertheless there is a Scottish flavour about a number of North-umbrian place names, even if the connection is sometimes a mistaken one. *Shotley* almost certainly describes the Clearing where a Scots-man lived: on the other hand *Shotton* near Newcastle is more likely to denote the Homestead on the Steep Hill. In the 'Verdict of the Assize of England touching the boundary of the Marches' it appears that 'in the bounds between the said town of Mindrum and the town of Shotton the Scots have lately ploughed and sown a little parcel of ground'. In this case *Shotton* is the Scotsmans' Homestead. Con-trariwise, there is little doubt that *Scotland Farm*, *Scotch Meadows* and *High Scotch Hall* are connected with a totally different kind of

Scot, namely the tax of that name. This was a 'municipal levy' which was made on everyone, according to their ability to pay. Where for any reason it was remitted, one was enabled to get off 'scot-free'.

Shoreston, near Bamburgh, was thought at one time to have had a Scottish connection. It is much more probable that it was the Hill where the Quick One lived—perhaps a noted runner. *Shoreswood*, *Shoresworth* and *Shoresdean* are different again for their meaning is, respectively, the Wood, the Enclosure and the Valley where there is a Steep Slope.

Yet a Scotsman was the originator of *Scotswood*, even if the connection was somewhat indirect, for it was in 1367 that Richard, son of John Scot, obtained permission to enclose the West Wood in Benwell which belonged to him.

Scotscoltherd (or Scotscoltard) marks the place just north of the Roman Wall where the Reivers from this side were wont to pause in the shelter of the ridge before gathering up the Horses or Herds that they had 'shifted' from the Scots. *Scots Gap*, like *Bloody Bush*, actually commemorates a Scottish raid. It was usual for the flocks in that district to be driven into a night-fold known as the Villains' Bog. This was a hollow suitably enclosed by a strong earth dyke and approached by a narrow Avenue, or Gap. It was at this opening to the night-fold that a famous battle with the Scottish mosstroopers took place, and it was to their repulse that the village owes is name.

A glance at the record of the Newcastle Assizes round about the year 1600 confirms the impression one gets that it was not only the Scots who made life difficult but the Northumbrians themselves, for they seem to have been a pretty rough lot. Indeed it appears to have been quite normal for gangs of 'gentlemen' to waylay, beat up or rob others of the same kind, or for individuals to indulge in what can only be described as petty thieving. In 1603, for instance, it appears that 'John Errington, gentleman, at Matfen made insult and affrey upon Mark Harryson, put him in fear of his life and robbed him of 30/- in money, a piece of linen cloth worth 20/- and 3 blue caps worth 12d. each'.

Murders were of almost daily occurrence and it is nothing to find such entries as one of 1595 where John Johnson of Whitfield, yeoman, and two others, were accused of murdering John Cragge of Towne Greene, when Johnson with 'a long fower squared pyked staffe value 2/- held in both hands pierced him through the guts with the said iron staff'. Indeed, for many years after the Union of the Crowns not only did border forays continue but the 'yeomen and gentry' whose homes were peel towers, their business farming and their hobby reiving, continued happily to attack each other as well as their counterparts on the other side of the Border.

NOTES

[10] smoke.
[11] Herd.
[12] Brindled.

CHAPTER 17

For stories of border forays and cattle raids in real profusion one must go to North Tyne where there lived (and still live) four clans, or graynes, whose name is for ever enshrined (if one can conscientiously use that word) in the annals of the Border.

First and, by common consent foremost, were the Charltons who had their headquarters at Hesleyside. Here it was that when the household and its manifold retainers and hangers-on were in need of fresh meat, the lady of the house placed on the breakfast table a dish which, when the cover was removed, was seen to contain a spur, the signal for a cattle raid into Scotland.

Another stronghold of the Charltons was *The Lee Hall*, that is to say the Stone-built House by the Pasture. Indeed nothing but a peel or a house built, like Bellingham Church, without timber was likely to survive the attention of the Scots, or even of one's neighbours, for very long. After a raid the mud-and-timber cottages could be rebuilt, but there had to be some permanent focal point for the community. In the fourteenth century this had been known as the Manor of Evelingham, the village of Eofa's people, but by 1604 as 'Leemalinge and Lee Hall' which 'were both the same thing'.

Here it was that a certain William Charlton lived, who had a long-standing feud with Lowes, the County Keeper, who lived at Walwick. The former seems to have had a summary method of dealing with civil servants for, managing to seize Lowes one day and to carry him off to Lee Hall, he secured him to the kitchen grate with a length of chain just long enough to enable him to eat at the servants' table. If it had not been for the giant Frank Stokoe of Chesterwood, there is no knowing how long the wretched man would have had to suffer this indignity.

The name Lee Hall, of course, is only one of many like *Leas Hall*, *Lea Crest* and *Lee Moor* that are connected with a Clearing or, later, a Pasture. The same word appears in *Kidland Lee*, the Pasture near Cydda's Land, and in *Mattilees* where Matta settled: also in *Notty Lees* where the Clearing was bald or Smooth and in *Roughlees* where it was just the reverse. *Rufflers Close* may also have started life as Roughlees so that the name would denote an Enclosure where the Pasture was Rough. The same idea of Roughness is indicated by the Clearing of *Rowley*; the Foot of the Hill at *Rowfoot*, the Hillside of *Rowside* and the Blind Valley of *Rowhope*.

The Old English 'geat' originally denoted a Gap so that *Portgate*, at the top of Stagshaw Bank, could mean the Gate in the Gap in the Roman Wall where Dere Street passes through, and (rather confusingly) it is the Gate that means the Gap and the Port the Gate. On the other hand there is another *Portgate* near Allendale Town where the meaning is surely the Market Road. Bearing in mind the Fair that was held there for many years, it is difficult to avoid concluding that the real derivation of the Stagshaw farm is the same. From a Gap it is easy to see how the word came to mean the thing which closed the gap—in other words a Gate, as in the Old English 'hlid-geat' (a swing-gate). The process even went a stage further so that in some instances the word came to mean the land to which access was closed by a gate, and so a Pasture as in *Horse Gate*[13], or *Bygate*—the Pasture enclosed by a Bight or Bend in the River.

It is difficult, if not impossible, in some cases to trace whether a name comes from this Old English word or from the Scandinavian 'gata', meaning a Way or Road, which we still use almost in the original sense when speaking of a man's way of walking as his 'gait'. When the men of North Tyne, therefore, gave their warcry of 'Tarset Burn and Tarret Burn, Hard and Heather-bred, Yet, Yet, Yet' they were just shouting 'Give way there'.

A good example of the confusion that the different derivations can produce is to be found at *Limestone Brae*, the Bank in Allendale where the old 'galloway track', or way along which the ponies passed laden with lead, used to be known as the Outgate. On the track stood a Toll-gate, marking the parish boundary, which was accordingly known as the 'Ootyett Yett'. Another such Toll-gate near Sparty Lea gave its name to *Gatehouse* and the same explanation presumably fits the farm of the same name near Bellingham that used to be known as 'Yate House in the Manor of Charlton Yate', and probably *Low Gate* near Hexham as well.

To return to North Tyne, however, and the 'foremost grayne'—in other words the Charltons—another of them, known as Bowrie Charlton, from the fact that he lived at *The Bower* (in other words the Cottage or Sheltered Place), has his own niche in local history. It was in the reign of Queen Anne that he quarrelled with Henry Widdrington of Buteland over a horse. They left the racecourse at the Doddheaps, near Bellingham, and fought it out; Bowrie killing his opponent. He escaped to Wharmley and finally received the royal pardon, but Widdrington's relations buried their relative in front of the Charlton's pew door in Bellingham church. The inscription read 'The Burial place of Henry Widdrington of Butland, Gentleman, who was killed by Mr William Charlton of Redesmouth February 23rd in the year of our Lord 1711'. This made it pretty certain that Bowrie could not decently go to church again.

Second only to the Charltons were the Robsons. A stone found at Falstone, and originating not later than the seventh century, bears the inscription 'Eomaer set this (cross) up for his uncle Hroethbert. Pray for his soul'. Robert, in the natural order of things, will have sired Robertsons and Robsons so that he may well have been the ancestor of the grayne. If he was cast in the same mould as his cattle reiving descendants the prayer will not have been ill-founded.

One of the Robson strongholds was the Hill by Bynna's Marsh, then known as Byndmire and now as *Bimmer Hill*. Another was *Leaplish* which in 1628 was the home of Matthew Robson whose wife Jane was accused at Newcastle Assizes of murdering her sister-in-law Mabell Robson by witchcraft. She must have been lucky to get away with it.

Here also took place a typical border foray. The Robsons were particular enemies of the Elliots of Liddesdale who, in 1611, in company with several Armstrongs and other cronies, descended upon Leaplish and committed what Sir William Fenwick described as 'the moste horrible and greevous outrage that ever hath been donne in my tyme within these partes' when 'about the number of three score and tenne persons, fiftee of them upon horsebacke, and the rest foot-men, all furnished either with long peeces, pistoletts, or launces, came to Lyonell Robson's house, in Leapelish ... and there cut downe his dwelling house with axes which they braught with them. And with their peeces killed one Lyonell Robson of the Smaleburne and a woman called Elizabeth Yearowe of Stannisburne and shott and hurt dyvers more, both men and women'. Indeed the casualty list included no less than three women as well as four men; eight others being 'shott with bullettes through their clothes but not hurte'.

Leaplish incidentally, marks the place on the Letch, or Slow-running Stream where there was a 'hlip', or Leaping-place. Stannis-burne was presumably the modern *Stannersburn*, the Stream with a Stony Ford, akin to *The High* and *Low Stanners* at Morpeth and elsewhere. Smaleburne is unlikely to have been the modern Smales which we have already encountered: rather is it the modern *Small-burn*, where there was a Narrow Stream.

Elizabeth Yearowe must have had something to do with Thomas Robson of Yearowe Hall who, the account of that famous raid goes on to state, was 'shott with one quarter shott in the fillettes of his backe, another quarter shott in his haunch and another great bullott shott through his Breeches and mist his skinne'. It is difficult to tell now whether the reference is to Yarrow or to *Yearhaugh*. If it is to the latter, the meaning is the Low Ground where there is a Fishery.

A 'yare' is the old name for a weir or dam to hold up salmon, forc-ing them to pass into a lock or trap. Fish, of course were, as ever, a valuable source of food and all the more so in view of universal abstinence from meat on Fridays and in Lent. It is no wonder that, at some time in the twelfth century, the men of Prudhoe were guilty of destroying the weir built by the inhabitants of Whickham because it prevented the fish from passing up-stream to their benefit.

It is probable that the same kind of thing was to be found at *Wylam*, for the name means the Village with a 'wile'. This Old Eng-lish word represented something wily, either a trick or a contrivance; what the French would call an 'appareil', which can be anything from a tin opener to a tank. The odds are that in this case, also, the appara-tus was a Fish-trap.

The corresponding article on dry land, namely an Animal Trap, is quite possibly the explanation for the Heap, or Structure, of Logs which is the meaning of *Chipchase*.

But, to return to the Robsons; it is recounted of them that, having a feud with the Grahams of Liddesdale, they drove a flock of the latter's sheep into North Tynedale. The sheep got their own back by infecting the Robsons' flock with scab, whereupon the Robsons returned to the fray, caught and hanged seven of the Grahams and warned the others that 'the neist tyme gentlemen cam to tak their schepe, they war no to be scabbit'.

There is an attractive legend explaining the origin of the name Dodds. On an occasion during the Seventh century when the Danes threatened Lindisfarne, the monks took the body of St Cuthbert and crossed to the mainland. After much wandering, their number was reduced to four whose sole supply of food was a salted horse's head and a cheese. One morning the cheese was missing: the monks, in high dudgeon, prayed that whoever had stolen it should be turned into a fox, and immediately a fox appeared out of the forest (though apparently no cheese). Curiously enough one Eilaf was missing. Putting two and two together, the brethren came to the not unnatural conclusion that Eilaf was the culprit but, repenting of their action, prayed to St Cuthbert to have him restored to human shape, which the Saint obligingly did. Ever afterwards Eilaf's family (one hopes not his descendants as such) were known as Tod or Dodd, signifying a fox. Smalesmouth and Yarehaugh, both of which we have already encountered, were among the possessions of this particular grayne.

Then there are the Milburns, taking their name from a Mill Stream, as at *Milbourne* where there used to be a Grange or Grain Farm belonging to the monks of Hexham Priory. Besides Roses Bower, the Milburns owned *The Combe* which takes its name from the Cam or Ridge on which it stands, as at *Adeycombe* near Rothbury, where someone called Aeddis may have settled, and at *Comb Hill* and the Heel of Land known as *Combey Heugh*.

It was Barty Milburn of The Combe who acquired such a reputation in the seventeenth century for strength and swordsmanship. One day he found his sheep missing so, with his friend Corbit Jack, he made off, past Blackburnhead and across the Carter into Scotland.

Failing to find their own sheep, they drove off some from Leatham but were overtaken near Chattlehope Spout. Corbit Jack was soon killed but Barty aimed a tremendous blow at one of the Scotsmen and 'garred his heid spang along the heather like an inion'. He then slew the other, collected both their swords, lifted Jack's body on to his back and, wounded as he was, drove the sheep home.

No chapter dealing with the rustling of cattle would be complete without the story of Dicky of Kingswood who had similar ideas. One day, on his way back from Newcastle, two fat beasts in a field near Denton Burn caught his eye. These he 'liberated' from their field and drove westward until he reached the Cumberland border where he sold them to a farmer. Fancying the look of the latter's horse, Dicky waited till nightfall and then made off with it. On his way home he encountered a man looking anxiously for a couple of beasts that had disappeared. 'I've seen two cattle answering that description' says Dicky 'but they're some distance away and you can't do the journey on foot: can I sell you a horse?' Delighted, the man buys the horse and, following the directions given to him, arrives at the Cumberland farm where he discovers the cattle peacefully grazing. Unfortunately the story ends there and history does not relate what happened when the two victims confronted each other.

The name *Kingswood*, the home of the hero of this story, must have referred to a Royal Forest, while *Denton* denotes a Homestead in the Dene or Valley.

NOTE

[13] A stint for one horse in a common pasture was also known as a horse-gate.

CHAPTER 18

FOR long enough it has been customary to think of the Border as a natural dividing line between peoples of totally different ancestry who could never have been expected to mix. Nothing could be further from the truth.

Although in the Celtic era there may have been little community of interest between the tribes north of the Tweed and those further south, this was by no means the case in Anglo-Saxon times. The settlement of what was to become Northumbria really began around the Humber and there seems to be considerable difference of opinion whether Northumberland, as such, was settled by these people or directly from abroad. In either case, two facts seem indisputable; first that the settlement took place from the sea inwards and, second, that the Celts put up such a spirited resistance that the Angles were for long enough confined to the coastal strip, and even to Lindisfarne alone.

Nevertheless, when once the invaders had gained a real foothold, it was not long before they had overrun not only the country south of the Tweed but a good deal of land to the north of it as well. Indeed by the time that Edwin became king of a united Northumbria, his northern boundary lay along a line joining the Firths of Forth and Clyde, beyond which the Picts were firmly entrenched. There seems little doubt that it was this same Edwin who founded the city of Edinburgh.

Generally speaking, therefore, the peoples of Northumberland and of the Scottish lowlands were, and are, of much the same stock. Yet there must have been tribal differences within the general pattern of settlement and it is these differences that have presumably led to the different pronunciations of the 'ingham' names. Even in this the

Tweed does not seem to have been the dividing line, but some boundary further south. This is the explanation for the pronunciation of *Chillingham*, which in 1231 was known as Chevelingham—the Village of Ceofel's People—and is pronounced with a hard 'g' like Coldingham on the Scottish side of the Border. Yet in the case of every other place in Northumberland with the same ending, from Eglingham to Eltringham, the 'g' is soft. Further south again, on Teeside, the pronunciation of Billingham returns to what is normal for the rest of England.

The inevitable result of this settlement of North East England and South East Scotland by tribes so akin to each other is that we speak much the same basic language, with differences largely of inflection. But that is not the only connection between what afterwards, through accident of politics much more than geography, became two peoples.

For long enough, the whole of North Tyne down as far as Chollerford formed part of the private estate of the Scottish kings, so that as late as 1263 we find William de Swynburne acting as Treasurer to Margaret, Queen of Scotland, and paying ten shillings rent to the Scottish crown for land in Halton and Halton Strothers.

It is a 'ceole' or Gorge that is the explanation of *Chollerford* and also of *Chollerton*, the Homestead by that same Ford, while *Halton* is the Homestead, as *Hawick* is the Farm, by a Look-out Hill.

In *Halton Strothers* we renew our acquaintance with Marshes, this time covered by Scrub, as in *Palmstrothers*; in *Haughstrother* (the Low Ground by the South Tyne) and in *High Struthers* in Allendale.

Then there is *The Strother Farm* at Holywell. In the Middle Ages a daughter of Del Strother, Lord of Lyham, married a Delaval and this may well have been the reason for connecting the name with a place that belonged to the Delavals and which has also been known as *Holywell Old Hall*. It was through the heiress of another Del Strother, this time in the fifteenth century, that the Loraine family came into possession of *Kirkharle*. *Harle* is one of the few places in Northumberland that is named after someone—in this case Herela—without addition of any other word, and to this was added the appellation Church, as at *Kirknewton*, where the del Strothers (or People of the Marsh) seem to have originated. This place appears in 1336 as The New Town in Glendale and the addition of the word

Church probably springs from the tradition that it was here that King Edwin married Ethelburga of Kent, in whose train came that same Paulinus who baptised so many at Holystone, and who used the River Glen for his earliest christenings.

The natural hazards to which Northumbrians used to be subject are shown up pretty clearly by a 'new stone set up in the place of an old one by Sir William Loraine Bart: in 1728. In memory of Robert Loraine his Ancestor who was barbarously murdered in this place by the Scots in 1483 for his good service to his Country against their thefts and Robbery. As he was returning home from the Church Alone Where he had Been at his private Devotions'. This stone, which still stands in the park at Kirkharle, may be contrasted with a later inscription in the Church, which reads 'Here lyes the body of Richard Loraine Esq. Who was a proper handsome man of good sense and behaviour: He dy'd a batchelor of an appoplexy walking in a green field near London October 26th 1738 in the 38th year of his age'.

But to return to the Scots in their more peaceful role, a further connection with Northumberland is to be found in the presence of the Baliol family at *Bywell*, the place that lies by a Stream in the Bight, or Bend, of the river. It was they who provided, in the shape of John Baliol, a king of Scotland who did homage to Edward I, whose influence had placed him on the throne, at the Black Friars Monastery in Newcastle.

It was of Bywell, also, that Roger North, the brother of the Lord Chief Justice, wrote when describing the latter's progress on the Northern Circuit in 1676. The roads in Northumberland, he said, were then so unsafe that there was a law that 'the tenants of the different manors of a barony must guard the judges thro' the territory. Out of it they would not go—no not an inch, to save the souls of them. They were a comical sort of people, riding upon negs, as they called their small horses, with long beards, cloaks and long broad swords, with basket hilts, hanging in broad belts, that their legs and swords almost touched the ground; and everyone in his turn, with his short cloak and other equipage, came up cheek-by-jowl and talked with my lord judge. His lordship was very well pleased with the discourse, for they were great antiquaries in their own bounds'.

In the days when William the Lion held the barony of Tindale it was *Wark on Tyne* that housed the Scottish Judges. As in the case of *Wark on Tweed*, the meaning of the name is 'weorc', or Fortification. In the first case the earthwork in question was the Man-made Hill of the 'Motte-and-bailey' castle, while in the second it was the Cam or Ridge extending towards Carham which was once thought to have been thrown up by man. Tradition has it that it was in the castle of Wark on Tweed that Lady Salisbury dropped her garter and Edward III picked it up, quieting the courtiers' giggles with the immortal words 'Honi soit qui mal y pense'.

Wark on Tyne has claims to have been the place once known as Scyteceastre (also ascribed to Chesters) where, typically, yet another assassination took place; this time of King Alfwald in 788. Not far away, of course, is *Shitlington*, the Homestead of Scyttel's People, while near Otterburn lies *Shittlehaugh* which, just to make matters still more confusing, is the Low Ground shaped like a Shuttle.

It is possible that William the Lion is commemorated in *Williamston* in Knarsdale which was once in his possession. Certainly it was the Homestead belonging to some William or other: the only question is which. Subsequently—that is to say in 1256—it belonged to a certain William Pratt, after whom it passed to yet another William, namely de Swyneburne.

Humshaugh (mentioned earlier in this chapter) is probably less well known for its Scottish connections, or for the fact that its name denotes Hun's Haugh (or the Low Ground by the river that was settled by Hun), than it is for its Paper Mill. Here it was that the forged banknotes were printed to be sent over to Flanders with the Duke of York's ill fated expedition of 1793, in order to embarrass Napoleon. It is probable that this was also the occasion, rather than the Battle of the Dunes in 1658, that led to the farm of *Dunkirk* being so named.

Another important influence in Northumberland for several hundred years was the Prince Bishop of Durham. Ever since the lands that had been given by St Oswald to Lindisfarne Priory passed to the Bishop of Durham, the latter had been the greatest landowner in the north. It would have been easy to say the greatest in the county, but this could be confusing for St Cuthbert's Lond, as the Shires of 'Norham and the Isles' and of *Bedlington* (named after the Homestead of Betla's people) were once known, was not considered, until 1844, as being part of Northumberland at all, but as North Durham. Thus it came about that in the old farm house at Elwick, which was replaced in 1864 by the present farm cottages, some used to sleep in Northumberland and some in the Palatinate, for the boundary between the two passed through the middle.

The capital of the northernmost shire, known when Sir Robert Ogle was its Sheriff, as the Counties of Norham and Eland, was of course, *Norham*. Once known as Ubbanford (Ubba's Ford), its name was changed to the North Settlement, presumably to distinguish it from Durham itself. It was here that the Bishop, whose power was second only to the king's, so far as the Northern Counties were concerned (and not always to his) held his exchequer. In other words, his Chancellor would sit at the chequer-board used to demonstrate to the illiterate the calculations that were being made when receiving their rents and payments.

Perhaps this change of name influenced that of another place in the shire, namely *North Sunderland*, which has managed so successfully to contradict itself. As early as 1176 it was known as Suthelande, in other words the Southern Land, presumably to differentiate it from Norham, though why this should have been neccessary remains a bit of a puzzle. Anyway, for some equally inexplicable reason it subsequently acquired another 'Land' at the end and then reappeared as Sutherlanlande. Presumably this came to be pronounced as Sunderland, and to be confused with the town of that name, so that North was added in an attempt to make a further distinction; thus completing a process which must have few equals for etymological idiocy.

Another force in the county in very early days was the Bishop of Hexham, who administered the lands subsequently known as Hexhamshire, which had been given to St Wilfred when he was Bishop of York. Such names as *Bishopside* and *Bishopfield*, signify respectively the Hill and Open Expanse belonging to the Bishop but, as the Bishopric of Hexham ceased to exist in 821, the reference is presumably to the Archbishop of York to whom his land reverted.

In 681 *Hexham* was known as Hagustaldes-ea, in other words the Water beside which Dwelt the Warrior, or Bachelor or, more precisely, the Younger Son who was not entitled to any part of the 'town' lands, and must make his own way in the world. Even after the bishopric had ceased to exist, the Canons of Hexham continued to enjoy considerable power, owning, as they did, land all over the south and west of Northumberland. That they were also of an independent turn of mind is shown by their reaction to the commissioners of Henry VIII when they came to dissolve the Priory. The monks barricaded the doors and lined the walls with armed men under the command of one of their number, the Master of Ovingham, in full armour, his bow bent with an arrow. From 28th September until 15th October 1536, they held out and nearly started a revolution in Tynedale.

Another feature of Hexham was the presence of flourishing glove-making and dyeing industries. *Okerland* for instance took its name from the Land that grew Ochre used in glove-making, while the Mallows used for dyeing were grown at the Farm of *Mollersteads* and presumably turned to account at *Dye House* next door.

Lindisfarne, which was not only the Cradle of Christianity in Northern England but itself the nucleus of the Bishopric of Durham, was originally Lindisfaran-eg, or the Island of the People of Lindsay. The latter, now forming the northern part of Lincolnshire, was once one of the Anglian kingdoms. Holy Island, then, was either a colony of these same people or of people who 'fared' to and fro from Lindsay. Presumably the Lindis channel separating it from the main land tooks its name from the island and not vice-versa. 'The Holy Islande', runs a fourteenth-century description, 'is situated within the sea ... and hath in the same a little borough towne all sete with fishers very poor'. But it had apparently a valuable rabbit warren.

Considering that the *Farne Islands* are not far away, one might have been forgiven for assuming that 'farne', which is common to both, was Old English for an Island. We have already seen that in the case of Lindisfarne it was something quite different, and the same is true here. Apparently Farne Island itself, when looked at from some angle or other, was reminiscent of a Fern.

Not only does another of the Farne Islands take its name of

Staple Island from the Pillars of Rock of which it consists, but *High Staples*, near Hexham, does the same, though whether in the latter case these were something natural, or arranged by man, is not known.

CHAPTER 19

ADMIRAL Collingwood once wrote about the beloved daughters that he had left behind in Northumberland: 'I am told that dress is out of fashion—that they have even left off petticoats— I hope to God my good girls will be able to make their way respectably through the world without petticoats—as it has pleased Him to make the climate so much warmer than it used to be'.

Warmer it may have been than it once was, but in a county that has never claimed to be particularly balmy there have always been, in the nature of things, certain places that were more than ordinarily cold and draughty. *Coldlaw* and *Coldside* must be particularly Cold Hills and *Cowden* a particularly Cold Valley, while one can readily imagine the wind blowing Cold across the Scrubby Swamp of *Coldstrother*. *Colt Crag* (once known as Kelly Quarter) and *Colt Park* look as if they might be explained in the same way while *Coldcoats* probably describes Huts or Shelters that were exposed to the Cold, rather than a place where one could shelter from it.

Cold Knuckles explains itself vividly enough while *Coldrife* seems to have been an even more popular name. Where we talk about being wakeful, our Northumbrian forbears talked about being 'wakerife'. It was natural therefore that they should so christen a place that was Full of Cold.

A name that is less obviously connected with the climate is *Catcherside*, which should delight the hearts of anyone who has read Stella Gibbons' 'Cold Comfort Farm', for this is almost exactly what Cold-cheer-side (of the Hill) describes. Yet *Catchburn*, where in the thirteenth century there stood the Hospital of Kacheborne, denotes the Stream where Caecca lived.

Perhaps more surprising than the allusions to Cold Places are those names which are descriptive of Cold Water, for what else did the settlers expect? There seem to be any number of places called *Coldwell* or *Caldwell*, alluding to Springs or Streams that are inordinately cold. Another such is *Calder*, denoting the Cald-ea or Cold Water of the Harelaw burn.

Names that are particularly deceptive in this connection are those like *Bleaklaw* and *Bleakhope* which denote respectively a Hill and Blind Valley that are Black rather than bleak. As in the case of Black Callerton and of the Hill at *Blakelaw*, this 'blackness' can be a description of soil where there are outcrops of Coal or, as in the case of the Hills that gave *Blackhalls* (near Kirkwhelpington) its name, and of the two mentioned earlier, it may denote Heather.

Peaty water, and streams that run in Shadow, also earn the title of Black: hence *Blackburn, Blackaburn*, the Gloomy Valleys of *Blagdon* and *Blagdonburn* and the Ravine of *Blackcleugh. Blackblakehope*, however, presents a certain problem for why should it be 'blacked' twice? The most likely explanation seems to be that here we are concerned both with Dark Water and with Heather at the same time.

The explanation of *Bleach Green* lies in none of the foregoing but in the old cottage industry where it was the practice to stretch the cloth on a patch of Grass in order to Bleach it.

Then there are the Windy Places. Windyhaugh we have already met but there are also such names as *Windy Side* and *Wandy Law*, both denoting Windy Hills, and *Wandysteads*, the Windy Steading or Farm.

Windy Walls describes the Remains or Foundations of someone else's building on a Windy Site. This use of 'walls' to describe the remains of an older settlement is comparatively common in Northumberland and is more generally associated with a personal name of Middle English origin. What probably happened was that land went out of cultivation with the demise (perhaps during the Black Death) of the occupant, or his inability to farm it. This, then would be 'Old Land' brought back into cultivation.

Places like *Dick's Old Walls* and *Walker Walls* admit of little explanation except to say that Dick and Walker would be the names of the new, rather than the old occupants, and that the latter would not necessarily be a fuller by trade, though he must have been descended from one.

Marley Cote Walls, near Slaley, was described in 1540 as Marrelcote Walls and in 1629 as 'Marlecoate alias Mallycoate Walls'. In 1288 Philip de Merlay appears as a 'tenant in Slaley' and it seems fair to assume that it was de Merlay (subsequently known, like all his family, as Marley) who occupied a place where there were the Remains of someone else's 'cot' or Shelter.

The name of Marley keeps cropping up in the history of the county and, one assumes, in some of our place names. *Marlish,* for instance, near Hartburn, was probably once Marley's Hall; just as *Corridge* was once known as Corrish or Corrie's Hall. Weight is lent to this theory by the fact that part of the road from Ulgham to Morpeth used to be called Marlish (Marley's) Gate after de Merlay, Baron of Morpeth.

Normally, one knows little or nothing about the origin of any particular walls. In the case of *Thompson's Walls,* however, we do. The place used to be known as Derecaster and subsequently as Antechester which, in turn, signified the remains of a Roman Camp marked by a Single Tree. American settlers might well have known it as Lone Tree Camp.

It might be imagined after all this that *Marldown* was also connected with the de Merlays, but this is not in fact the case for it seems probable that the real meaning is the Hill where there was a 'mael', that is to say a Mark or Cross as at *Meldon.*

'Gemaere' or 'maere', the Old English word for a Boundary, appears in *Mardon,* the Hill and *Marden,* the Valley, on the Boundary. In the days when farms were still being increased by clearing woodland and improving swamps that appeared to belong to no one in particular, the question of boundaries was not tremendously important. As the countryside came increasingly into cultivation, however, the question of where one man's land finished, and another began, became more and more a matter of debate. And so sprang up the custom of riding the boundaries (or beating the bounds) at regular intervals. As late as 1840 the county was still divided into baronies and the bounds were being ridden with representatives of all the interested landowners being present.

The procedure was for the whole party to ride (and walk) from boundary stone to boundary stone, or currock to currock, and where someone claimed the line should run in a different direction or that a stone had been shifted or removed, he would walk 'his' line until meeting up again with the others. Afterwards there would be an assize at which evidence would be taken from the oldest inhabitants or other interested parties and the proper line would be marked again.

In this connection it is worth quoting at some length the official report of the riding of the boundaries of Blanchland Common in 1793. The participants certainly seem to have done themselves well. 'Then there was a halt for about half an hour when each of the Runners got Bread and Beef and a glass of spirits and Gingerbread was thrown amongst all the company present and scrambled for. And here William Horsley one of the runners was taken up by two men who knocked his Bottom, alias his Backside against the Warlow Pike Stones until they knocked down the top of them—and after three acclamations from all the company we proceeded from Warlow Pike in a North West Direction for near half a mile when we crossed the head road near Emley Well'.

Down the Embley burn they went and up the Devil's Water and across the moors to Baybridge where 'everyone was entertained with Beef Tongue Hams Bread and Ale and the Runners with the like and with Spirits, Figs Raisins and Gingerbread'.

At another Bounder Stone the Runners got Cold Mutton, Bread, Wine and Brandy and at 5.0 p.m. the whole party returned to Blanchland and were 'plentifully entertained' by the Lord Crewe Trustees. The Runners apparently included Thomas Makepiece of Cowbyers, aged 27, James Proud of the same, aged 27, and Michael Hudson of Blanchland, aged 9!

On the second day 'John Champion of Jeffrey's Rake aged 55 was taken up by two men and his Bottom, alias his Backside was thumped or knocked against the Currock five or six times'. (This was at the Dead Friar Currock which marks the grave of an itinerant preacher.)

Subsequently the party came to a heap of stones whose name was unknown to them, so they called it Adams Currock 'in compliment to the Steward of the Manor of Blanchland'—a good example of a place name actually in the making. This word currock, meaning a cairn or heap of stones, is fairly common in Northumberland and, indeed, in the North generally. It is one of the few Celtic words still in regular use, being derived from 'carroc' a Rock. *Watch Currock*, therefore, takes its name from the pile of stones where Watch was kept.

Yet another name for a boundary is, of course, a March, which gives us names like *March House* near Wylam, and *Throckley Marsh* which lies, in fact, almost at the top of the Fell and is entirely un-connected with a marsh. The Scottish rendering of March is Merse, as in the case of the Merse of Berwick which borders on that curious corner of Northumberland, north of the Tweed, that always looks on the map as if it should be in Scotland and is not. The reason, of course, is that it comes within the boundaries of Berwick-upon-Tweed which changed hands so often between English and Scots, sometimes in the most revolting circumstances, that in the end there must have been some doubt who it really did belong to. Certainly, mention used to be made of 'England, Scotland and Berwick-upon-Tweed'. Hence also the story (which, if it is not true, it should be) that while Berwick was included in the proclamation of the Crimean War, its name was omitted from the subsequent peace treaty, so that its inhabitants are still technically at war with the Russians.

Halidon Hill and Camphill have already been mentioned in con-nection with the battle, but there still remain a number of farms clustered about with curious names some of which are difficult to explain. *Baitstrand* was called after a 'bass' or Cowshed on the Shore of the burn. Cumberland Bower next door, and Gainslaw, we have already encountered. *Fairney Flatt* is no doubt the Flat ground covered with Bracken and *Scuddylaw* the Hill where the soil is of Little Value, while *Baldersbury Hill* is likely to have marked the site of Baeldhere's Stronghold.

Then we come to those delightful twins, *Steps o' Grace* and *Conun-drum*. The former may have had some connection with Stepping Stones over the little burn nearby, but the name Conundrum is liter-ally a puzzle—perhaps it was meant to be! *Sanson Seal*, where the ashtree stands to which Edward III tied his horse before Halidon, is shown on Armstrong's map of 1769 as Sons and Seal, which is no help to anyone. In view of the Sele, or Marshy Stream nearby, the most probable explanation seems to be Samson's Stream, unless the allusion is to Sallows—the scrubby willows that grow in such a place.

CHAPTER 20

W HEN Camden visited Northumberland in 1604, he reported that 'Here every year round about in the wastes as they term them ... you may see ... a martial kind of men who from the month of April lie out scattering and summering (as they term it) with their cattle in little cottages here and there which they call sheal or shealings.... For their shieldinge grounds they doe begyn and end by agreement among themselves according as the season falleth out'.

By the year 1700, or thereabouts, the shieling system, of which we have already heard a good deal, must have been coming to an end for, because of constant division between sons, cleared land had become sufficiently scarce to make it necessary for the areas in question to be farmed more intensively. Nevertheless, there were large areas such as Rothbury forest still to be won for agriculture, and the population probably still did not exceed fifty thousand at the outside. Apart from Newcastle, which was one of the most important centres in the country, only a tiny proportion lived in the towns.

After the accession of James V to the throne of England, it had been no longer necessary for the Wardens of the Marches to keep a muster roll of 'men able in horse and harness' and men 'able, wanting horse and harness' upon whom they could call at short notice to repel a Scottish invasion. Gradually the Mosstroopers had begun to turn their hands to other kinds of thievery or even to no thievery at all. Gone also were the days when a ballad maker could write:

> I saw cum marching owre the knows
> Fyre hundred Fenwicks in a flock.

as at the Raid of the *Redeswire*. This was the classic encounter which arose out of a peaceful meeting of the English and Scottish Wardens and their followers at the 'swire' or neck of land at the head of Redesdale. Indeed it would be tempting to suggest that the Red one (in other words the River Rede) was so named because of the English and Scottish blood that must have so often dyed its waters. In fact, of course, the name is much older and must surely arise from its peaty colour. *Redeswood* describes the Wood nearby, as *Redesmouth* of course describes its Mouth, yet *Ridsdale* presumably takes its name from the Valley of that Reddish stream that flows into the Rede.

All is not Red, however, that would appear so. Near Haltwhistle, for instance, lies *Redpath* (there is another near Rothley) and there is little doubt that the derivation of the name is identical to that of *Ridpath*, near Hartburn. The Roman Road, known here as the Maiden Way but elsewhere as the Devil's Causeway, passes through the farm and explains why it was christened the Ridded, or Cleared, Path. This same idea of Riddance which we have met before in such names as Riding Mill and Hardriding appears once more in *Riddlehamhope*, the Blind Valley where the land has been Cleared for a Village.

Yet another place that may fall into this category is *Redshaw Foot*, which has been described in its time as Redeshaw, Roachy Foot and even (in 1663) as Rotchelle Foot. The most likely explanation, once more, is that it lay Below a Copse that had been Ridded or Cut Down.

But to return at last to the Fenwicks, it seems to be fairly well established that they took their name from *Fenwick* (the Farm by the Marsh) near Stamfordham. The same marsh, or part of it, was known once as Maeth's Fen from which *Matfen* takes its name, while the farm of *Matfen Piers* commemorates not the Roman Milecastle that stood close by but the Pillars of the gates which opened on to the main drive to Matfen Hall.

Fenton, the Homestead by the Marsh, is another such name, as are *Fenrother*, the Clearing by the Marsh, and *Shadfen*, the place where it was Shallow. Mousen and Pressen we have already encountered: there is also *Mason*, denoting that part of Prestwick Carr that was known as Maerheard's, and afterwards Murdo's, Fen.

The Fenwick family have left their name, in turn, at places like

Fenwickfield, the Open Expanse called after a thirteenth-century Rector of nearby Simonburn, and also *Fenwick's Close*, near Backworth, the land which, when Enclosed, passed to another of that name. There is another *Fenwick* near Belford, the Farm by the same Marsh that has given the Village of *Fenham* its name. The existence both of *Fenwick Granary* and of *Fenham Granary* is probably explained by the fact that the Monks of Holy Island used to farm at Fenham, and owned a mill and granary there.

This use of words such as Granary and Dairy to distinguish farms which might otherwise have shared the same name was presumably made necessary by the enclosure of more and more land, particularly that which was held in common, and of which we will hear more later. In some cases these farms were known as, for instance, *Cheswick Buildings*, *Acomb Buildings* and *Allerwash Buildings*. Others as *Longhirst Dairy* or *Hemelspath Dairy* (which was the Dairy Farm near the Steep Path where there was a Cattle Shelter). The word Hemmel which, of course, is still with us, appears again in *Red Hemmels* and *Black Hemmels* which presumably took their names from the colour of their roofs.

The word Barn is really a corruption of the Old English 'bere-aern' or Barley Building, and it is probably in this sense that *The Hall Barns* should be construed—that is to say as the Demesne Granary of Simonburn. The same applies to *Buston Barns* and *Bilton Barns*, connected with the manors that were called after Buttel's Hill and Billa's Homestead, respectively, and also to *Barns Farm* and *Barnhill*. *The Rope Barn*, on the other hand, presumably marks the Building in which Rope was twisted.

The accession of James I did not only remove the fear of large-scale warfare in Northumberland but, as Hodgson puts it 'After the Union of England and Scotland ... men withdrew from the protection of castles, fortalices and villages and waste lands and commons began to be divided and a new class of names given to new settlements, such as Blinkbonny, Brandy Well Hall, Breadless Row, Click-em-in, Cold Knuckles, Delicate Hall, Delight, Fell-him-down, Glower-o'er-him, Maccaroni, Make-me-Rich, Mount Hooley, Philadelphia, Pinch-me-near, Portobello, Quality Corner, Skirlnaked and numerous others equally fanciful'.

Hodgson may well be forgiven for regarding all these names as 'fanciful', as are many other farm names in the county, but, as will be shown, there are good reasons for some of them. *Blinkbonny* may have a comparatively modern name but the site must have been inhabited for more than two thousand years before the Union: indeed in 1856 gold ring-money from the early Bronze Age was discovered there. The farm derives its name from the splendid view that it affords of the Till valley. *Blawearie* near Eglingham might conveniently be explained as Sick-of-the-Wind on the same basis as warweary, but better still by the North Country use of 'weary' as meaning troublesome. Howard Pease used to tell a story of his visit to Bewcastle churchyard where he commented to the sexton on the disproportionate number of women's names appearing on the tombstones and asked why there were so few men represented. 'What happened the men?' the sexton replied. 'Wey, the men were aa' hangit at weary Carlisle.' Blawearie has been described as 'resting on a green pocket handkerchief on the top of the hill ... all around it was heather, heather and more heather, far as eye could reach'. No wonder the wind is troublesome.

Brandy Well Hall, as we have seen, has a perfectly sensible explanation. Breadless Row (or rather Breadless Raw) is now just known as *The Raw* and is in Redesdale. Raw, meaning a Row (of houses) appears over and over again in our place names and survives also in the Pit Raas of Tyneside. Often the word Raw is to be found coupled to some adjective that expresses distaste. *Bagraw*, for example, describes a Beggarly Row of Houses though it was originally thought to derive from the so-called Badgers who were itinerant Dealers in corn, butter and other foodstuffs. It was in 1693 that action was taken in Northumberland against 'all badgers, drovers and higlers that have not taken lycence as also those that keepe guns or grayhounds (not being qualified) and against all those that keepes nettes and junckettes to distroy the young fry of salmon'.

Ratten Raw which appears in various places and in various guises in Great Britain has been explained in so many different ways and with such a wealth of corroborative detail that one can do no less than mention some of them. In the case of Rotten Row in London, the name has been explained in five different ways at least. Perhaps the best of the five is that it formed part of the old 'Route du Roi' or Royal Route which the Plantagenet Kings used when riding from their Palace of Westminster to hunt in the royal forests. Curiously enough, this explanation is on all fours with the theory advanced in Scotland to explain a similar name, that it comes from the Gaelic Rathad-an-Righ, the King's Highway.

It is more likely, however, that in Northumberland Ratten is just the word 'raton' meaning Rat-infested. The Raw part of the name would, as usual, represent the Row of Houses which must have been quite a normal feature of the little 'towns' that have in so many cases become submerged in modern farms. Perhaps most likely of all is the explanation that is also most obvious; namely that the houses in question were 'primitive, Rotten dwellings of clay, wood and thatch as opposed to the stone-built Raw of farm places where the servants reside'. It is perhaps worth mentioning at this point that *Rothill* has no particular connection with poverty but takes its name from the 'roth', or Clearing, that crowned its Hill.

About 1700 *Rattenraw* near Haydon Bridge was described as 'now a good farm house, formerly a cluster of old peels' and spelt, in the same account, Row Town Row. *Raw Green* describes a Grassy Spot where there was a Row of houses, while *The Raw* near Longframlington appears in earlier days as Ecklesrowe, the Row by the Oak Clearing.

About the same time as Breadless Row there was a farm in existence known as *Breadless Straw* where it was said that the farmer could not grow enough corn to make himself a crowdy[14] for breakfast. The same idea of land being too poor to grow corn appears in yet another verse inspired by the virtues of Wallington:

> *Harnham was headless, Bradford breadless,*
> *Shaftoe picked at the craw.*
> *Capheaton was a wee, bonny place,*
> *But Wallington bangs them a'.*

Presumably Harnham was not so much without a head as without heed of the future, or was there, in fact, no Laird at the time? Odd things seem to have happened at this place, which was acquired at about the time of which we are speaking by a family rejoicing in the name of Winkle, or Wrinkle, so that we find a Griffin Winkle figuring in local history. So also (but later on) did Catherine Babington, wife of the squire, and daughter of Sir Arthur Haselrig. As a militant dissenter she had a long-standing quarrel with Mr Foster, the Vicar of Bolam, and persuaded the blacksmith's son to pull him out of the pulpit. This resulted in the parson excommunicating both of them and refusing to bury the lady not only in the church, which he had a perfect right to do, but also in the churchyard, which he had not. This is why Dame Babington finished up in the garden. The name *Harnham*, incidentally, describes a Homestead in the Horn or Corner of Land.

Documents of the fifteenth century and earlier are full of 'broad' places, such as Le Brade-schawe, meaning the Wide Copse and Le Brade-gate, the Wide Road, as well as plenty of Brad-meadows and Brad-flats but *Bradford*, meaning the Wide Ford, is one of very few such names left on the map. It must be a long time since it was judged incapable of producing decent crops.

It is rather more understandable that *Shaftoe*, the Shaft-shaped Spur of the Hill, provided few pickings,[15] owing to the rocky nature of the land overlying the crags. The same could hardly have been true of the Level (if Short) stretch of ground nearby, which in consequence is known as *Shortflatt*.

Heaton, now part of Newcastle, denotes (like *Hetton*) a High Homestead and this is also the explanation of *Capheaton* which in 1274 was known as Great Heaton to differentiate it from Little Heaton and particularly from *Kirkheaton* where a Church was built. Subsequently Great became latinised and reappeared as Cap or Chief, from 'caput' a Head. If Algernon Swinburne, the poet, had not spent so much time staying with his cousins there, there is no doubt that the saga of Northumberland would have been immeasurably poorer for no one has ever surpassed him in singing the county's praises. Another High Homestead, but on a Steep hill, is *Stickle Heaton* near Cornhill.

But this has taken us a long way from Hodgson and his fanciful names. *Click-em-in*, sometimes wrongly spent as 'inn', seems to have been a popular fancy. To Click is good Northumbrian for snatch, having much the same association as 'that deadly poaching instrument, the cleek'. It is possible, of course, that there were farms where one hoped, as it were, to rake in the shekels but it seems more likely that they were connected with Bringing in the Cows, as in the Scottish poem in which 'the third cow he cleikit by the heid'. It is only fair to add that, quite apart from farms, there has been more than one inn called Click-em-inn, where the name is supposed to reflect the coachmen's instructions to 'click in' the horses of the mail coach.

Cold Knuckles is indeed a Cold Spot (in Allendale) but is pretty well ruined now. Delicate Hall as we have seen is not so much fanciful as a normal corruption. It is possible, of course, that the same applies to *Delight* or is it one of those 'hopeful' names like another popular one—*Make-me-rich*? Certainly it seems to make more sense to give a place this kind of name rather than (say) *Extremity* or *Necessity* which used to exist in Hulne Park, and whose names are described by Tate, the historian of Alnwick, as 'jocular'. The real question is who gave these two their names, for whereas up to, and possibly including, medieval times, it seems to have been the neighbours who did the christening, we have now reached a point in history when names were bestowed by the owner, or at least the occupier.

Fell-him-down, like *Switch-her-down*, is now no more, except that the latter has left behind it Switcher Dene near Wandy Law. Could these names have been the sequel to the clearing of some fresh piece of forest, or was Switch-her-down, like its namesake near Middleton Hall, the haunt of a witch?

Glower-o'er-him is the modern *Glororum*. No explanation is so far forthcoming why the farm of that name near Morpeth should wish to 'glower o'er' anyone but there is an excellent explanation for the name of the one near Bamburgh. Its story begins in 1095 when Robert Mowbray, Earl of Northumberland, was unwise enough to plunder four of William Rufus' ships which were returning from Norway with cargoes of timber. The King, justly incensed, travelled the length of England with his army and besieged the Earl in Bamburgh Castle but (not surprisingly) without success. Accordingly he left part of his army in position and departed. Before doing so, however, he built on a neighbouring slope a wooden tower, known as a

Malvoisin, or Bad Neighbour, from which his men could overlook the castle. And so Glower-o'er-him was born.

Philadelphia, Maccaroni (called after the pit of that name) and *Quality Corner* are no longer with us but *Portobello*, the echo of a battle fought in 1739, still exists near Haltwhistle, while Mount Hooley and its various Hollytree relations have already been dealt with. *Skirlnaked* is well named, from its position, Shrieking (or Stark) Naked.

That leaves us, so far as Hodgson is concerned, with a further visit to Pinch-me-near, or at any rate to Fallodon West Farm as it now is. *Fallodon*, itself, denotes a Hill that has been Ploughed or Broken Up. The Old English 'fealu' has, in fact, several shades of meaning.

> Soldier, what do you see
> Lying so cold and so still?
> Fallowfield Fell at night
> And the stars above the Hill.

Those unforgettable lines by Wilfred Gibson, the Hexham poet, refer to a place the meaning of which is the Open Expanse that is Yellow, and no one who has seen the Fell at *Fallowfield* when the gorse is out is likely to disagree. The interesting thing is that there must have been gorse there for a thousand years or more.

In *Fallowlees* near Rothbury, which used to be a fair sized village, Fallow is used in yet another sense in that the place would not grow anything. It was here that William Veitch, the famous Covenanter, came to hide when he had made the countryside too hot to hold him. He had come to the wrong shop, however, for he was surrounded by Roman Catholic neighbours who 'did stir up the Lord Whiterington (Widdrington) to mar some small meetings he had'. In 1541 Fallowlees was described as 'having soylle or ground there of blacke covered with heather and lynge unprofytable for pasture', so it is the Uncultivable Clearing(s).

An Old English word that could possibly be confused with Fallow is 'fag' which is to be found in *Fawdon* (the variegated Hill) in *Fawns* (the variegated Ness or Headland) and probably in *Fawcett* (the variegated Hillside).

Another name that one might imagine to be fanciful is *Velvet Hall* (near Berwick) but it is equally probable that it is a corruption of Foul-flete, meaning a Dirty Stream; in fact the Allerdean Mill burn. The word 'flete' was more often used to describe a Tidal Stream so that *Fleetham* is the Village by such a Stream, in this case the burn called the Long Nanny that flows directly into the sea.

Tone Hall is a name much older than it sounds. In 1296 it was known as Tolland, the Land where Toll was paid. It was a Miss Hodgshon of Tone who, with the Misses Swinburne of Capheaton, acted as despatch riders for the 'rebels' during the '15 and shrewdly reported that although General Tom Forster quite looked the part on his big black horse, he was a 'pig-headed fool'. How right she was.

Nor is *Thrum Mill* so odd as it may seem. Thrum is a good old Northumbrian word for a drumming noise, or the purring of a cat, so it is not an unsuitable name for the gorge in the Coquet nearby. 'It's gan to be bad weather', say the Locals, 'hark hoo the Thrum's roaring'.

It is a wonder that Hodgson did not mention *Bakethin*, a name that surely sounds comical enough in all conscience; yet it has nothing to do with cookery; the real definition, without much doubt, being the Thorny Back, or Ridge.

Then there are two places in the north of the county, known as *The Ark* and *Luckenarks*. Now the word 'ark' can, for all relevant purposes, mean one of two things; either a Chest (Kist or Bin) or a Mountain Pasture. 'Lucken' means, in Scotland, Locked or Secure while further south its meaning becomes almost the exact opposite, namely Wide or Spacious. But any theory that The Ark is a Mountain Pasture does not fit the case while it is most unlikely that Luckenarks was the place where there was a Locked Corn Bin. There the matter must rest for the moment, but it is impossible to resist the temptation of quoting an instance of the use of the word Ark (latin 'archa') to mean a chest. When Scottish reivers broke into the house of Robert Unthank at Melkridge, they are alleged to have shut his daughter Alicia up in an ark!

Robert's family must have come from one of the places known as *Unthank*, of which there are several in Northumberland and elsewhere. They were not, as might be supposed, called after the thankless nature of their soil but after the form of their original tenure. They had in fact been occupied 'unthances' or Without Leave—in other words by a Squatter. *Unthank Square*, in particular, is worth looking at more closely for, in the days when no self-respecting Northumbrian would have dreamt of calling a Cuckoo anything but a Gowk, this was known as Cuckhold's Square.

Melkridge, where Robert Unthank lived, is one of many farm names descriptive of the value of their Grass. In this case it must have been good enough for cows to milk on, as in the case of *Milk-hope*, the Blind Valley with Rich Grass.

The same reasoning applies, and perhaps with added force, to *Butterknowes, Butterlaw* and *Butterwell* which describe the Hillocks, Hill and Stream where the grass was good enough to produce Butter. *Butterhaugh* would be Low Ground of the same nature but *Butter-wick* the Farm where Butter was made as a speciality (just as Cheswick was the Farm where Cheese was made). Yet *Cheeseburn* had not necessarily anything, either directly or indirectly, to do with cheese-making but was probably named after a Gravelly Stream— in other words the Pont. The same applies to *Chiselways Hall*, once known as Chiselly Hall, which must surely take its name from the Gravel banks in the North Tyne nearby.

NOTES

[14] Porridge.

[15] The reference is, in fact, to a long-standing argument between Shaftoes and Crasters (Craw-cesters).

CHAPTER 21

THERE is an old rhyme that runs:—

Dowly Dotland stands on the hill,
Hungry Yarrish looks at it still.
Barker House's a little below.
There's mokes i' the cairn[16] at Hamburn ho'.

All these are, of course in Hexhamshire. *Dotland* which, according
to the rhyme is lowering and gloomy, appears in 1160 as Dotoland
and it is anybody's guess whether the place was called after Dote or
a female called Dota. What is pretty certain is that either would be
Scandinavian in origin. Places called after women are fairly uncommon in Northumberland, but *Eddysbridge* is really Edith's Bridge
and *Eadsbush* may have been called after a lady of the same name.
In 1547 the latter was known as Edesmedowe and it is perhaps not
too late to observe that the Old English 'bysc', which is the origin of
Bush, also denoted a Thicket and it is in this sense that most of our
'bushy' names should be considered.

Yarridge we have already encountered and *Hamburn Hall* is called
after the Stream by the Village or Homestead (just as *Hampstead*,
near Corbridge, means the Homestead itself). *Barker House*, however,
is one of those places like Walk Mill, that is associated with a particular trade; in this case the Tanners whose Company in Newcastle and
elsewhere were known as the Barkers.

Not far from Dotland stands a farm with the curious name of
Loadman. This may once have been Ladmannisgate—the Lademan's
Pasture—and must have been the residence of a man who showed
the Lade, or Way, and therefore a Guide. Another useful member
of the community is commemorated by *Salmon Field* and *Salmons-*

well, the Expanse and the Spring, respectively, beside which lived a man called Salmon. Whether he was in fact a Suhlman or Ploughman we do not know but there is no doubt that he must have been descended from one. The same kind of query applies also to *Vinter's Hall*, near Haltwhistle, for this was the old word for a Vintner, whose Company may well have owned the land in question. Of *Brixter Hill* we can be more positive: it marks the spot where Brick-makers worked. In point of fact the making of bricks was by no means a common occupation in Northumberland until perhaps the seventeenth century. The Romans, of course, used to make a thin brick, rather like a tile, but after they retired from the scene no bricks at all were used in England until the fourteenth century when their importation from Flanders began. Where there was plenty of stone and timber to be had for building, as was the case in Northumberland, there was little point, anyway, in looking elsewhere.

It might be thought that *Taylorburn*, in Allendale, if it were not connected with a trade, was a corruption of Tail o' the Burn which would fit its location, like *Yont-the-Cleugh* which simply describes a farm on the Far side of the Ravine. In reality the place owes its name to the Taylor family, as does *Slaterfield*, near Simonburn, to the Slaters. Yet *Harperton* is unquestionably the Homestead of a Harper.

From actual trades it is, indeed, an almost imperceptible step to family names because so many of the latter arise out of the former. *Saddler's Hall*, for instance, and *Draper House*, were each probably called after a person of that name, as was *Gardener's Houses* at Dinnington where in 1663 a Robert Gardner was assessed for taxes.

Proctor Steads is a tricky name to derive, not so much because there is too little evidence but because there is too much. This is the farm that used once to be known as Dunstan Tower. In 1274 the living of Embleton, nearby, was bestowed by Earl Edmund, the younger son of Henry III, on Merton College, Oxford. The Earl subsequently revoked the gift but the College was not prepared to take this reverse lying down. For no less than sixty years they kept up the struggle, each of the parties appointing a priest to the living. History does not relate where the money came from to pay the two of them—perhaps there were sufficient pickings for both—but after all this had been going on for some years, Merton sent their Proctor north to bring the matter to court. The jury of local priests, however, were too frightened of the Earl's bailiff to bring in a verdict against him. In the end, Merton won their case and hold the living of Embleton to this day.

Another living held by the college is *Ponteland*, a place that takes its name from the fact that, before Prestwick Carr was drained, the River Pont used to flood to such an extent as to leave the village on an Island. Hence, also the Manor of Eland and *Eland Hall*. The name of the river in turn, derives from the Celtic 'pant' meaning a Valley.

It might seem reasonable to suppose that when Merton's Proctor was at Embleton he lodged at the house in question which, in turn, acquired his title as its name. Unfortunately this theory does not hold water. Dunstan Tower, which is understood (on his own authority) to have been the birthplace of that most famous of medieval scholars Duns Scotus ('the Scotsman'), was inhabited from the thirteenth to the end of the seventeenth century by a family bearing the delightful name of Wetwang, indicating that they came from a Wet Field. In 1705 it was exchanged by one John Proctor with the Craster family for property elsewhere; by which time it must have been rebuilt, for over the front door appears the inscription 'J.P.1652'. Hence also the name Proctor Steads.

So much for Dunstan Tower: *Dunstanburgh* itself has not, as might have been expected, any connection with St Dunstan but denotes the Stronghold on the Hill of Rock. As Winston Churchill might have said: some Stronghold, some Rock. It seems likely that *Dunstan Wood*, near Corbridge, also derives its name from a Rocky Hill.

But to return to family names: not far from Dunstanburgh lies *Christon Bank* which is called after the Quaker family that first enclosed it. *Selby House* grew out of land enclosed by the Selbys, who owned so much round Biddlestone, where the old mansion provided the original of Osbaldistone Hall for Scott's Rob Roy. *Biddlestone* itself was once thought to derive its name from the beetle-stones which used to be employed in Laundry work. That it had nothing to do with anything so exotic is apparent from the original spelling, which was Bitnesden or Bitlisden. In other words it was the 'botl', or

Building, in the Valley.

Another name in which the same word appears is *Budle* which denotes just 'botl' or Dwelling; no more and no less. This would seem
to be rather like christening one's place of abode 'House', and therefore to lack somewhat in originality. The explanation would seem
to be that in the days when these places first earned their names the
normal dwelling was built of timber, mud and turf, and was only
just sufficient to exclude the elements, and no more. A solid house,
perhaps with some stone in it, would rank as something quite special
that had been 'builded' rather than just thrown together.

Another example is *Bolton*, literally the Homestead with a Building but more probably, in practice, that part of the village where the
houses stood, or even where the Manor House stood. Yet another is
Lorbottle which was originally Leofhere's Dwelling and whose inhabitants subsequently earned a reputation for eccentricity doubtless
quite undeserved. In a survey of the Earl of Oxford's estates in 1724,
for instance, it was recorded that 'Lorbottle is divided at present into
two parts, the East and West ends ... The tenants of the east end
farm the west end and the tenants of the west end farm the east end'.

But worse was to come, for the villagers came to be known as the
Kebs of Lorbottle who were noted as much for the depth of their
stupidity as for the size of their appetites. It was alleged, for example,
that they were never aware that it was raining until they saw the
drops in the pond, appropriately known as Puddle. If several of them
sat on a fence they did not know which were their own legs and feet
and which were their neighbours'. They tried to build a wall round
the cuckoo to stop it flying away (this seems to have been a pretty
widespread accusation). And when they caught an eel, not knowing
what to do with it, they threw it into Puddle in order to drown it.

But to return to surnames, the Donkin family seem to have left
their mark on the farms of the county with *Donkinrigg*, near Rothley, that was originally Duncan's Rigg or Ridge, and *Donkin's Houses*
near Ponteland, that appears in the eighteenth century as Doncan's
or Duncan's House. The name Duncan, from which Donkin has
evolved, seems to be a very old one, having been recorded as such in
the thirteenth century together with names like Urkil and Uchtred
which are no longer with us.

Donkley Wood, however, has a totally different derivation for it is one of the many 'dun' or Hill names. In this particular case the meaning is a Hill, part of which forms a Cliff. *Dunsall* and *Dinley* are two more of the same sort, the first probably describing a place in the Shelter of a Hill and the second a Clearing on a Hill.

With *Dunsheugh*, however, we return once more to surnames, for this was the Spur of a Hill where Dunn lived, just as *Dunslawholme* denotes Low-lying ground by Dunn's Hill.[17] A man called Sproat once occupied *Whittonstall Sproats* and the Turpin family *Turpin's Hill*, near Heddon-on-the-Wall. As far back as 1242 the Turpins appear as considerable landowners in that particular part of the world and in 1290 Richard Turpin is to be found fighting, and winning, a great lawsuit against the Prior of Tynemouth in order to settle the boundary between the Turpins' land at Houghton and that of the Prior at Wylam.

Although pronounced differently, *Houghton* near Heddon-on-the-Wall and *Long Houghton* near Alnmouth both refer to a Homestead on the Heugh or Spur of a Hill. *Haughton*, however, is pronounced differently again for it was originally the Homestead in the Haugh, or Low-lying Ground.

There is, of course, a further trade to be discussed in connection with our place names, and one that had a big part to play in Border warfare particularly; namely that of the Smith. He it was who plied his trade, or perhaps did a little farming, in the Low Ground of *Smeatshaugh*, while *Smiddywell Rigg* takes its name from the Ridge above the Stream where his Smithy was.

Smeafield, moreover, is the Smith's Field, but what kind of a field? The answer is that it all depends on the date of the name. Prior to the Black Death in 1348 the word 'feld' meant an Open Space, or Expanse, larger than a Clearing; a meaning which has survived in (for instance) Flodden Field, the Field of the Cloth of Gold and the military expression 'in the field'. With the enclosures of land carried out by landowners (including particularly the Monasteries) after the Black Death, the word gradually assumed the meaning of an Enclosure or Field as we know it.

It is in the earlier sense that we should interpret some of the Fields

of the extreme south-east of Northumberland, where names with that
ending are particularly numerous on the higher ground. *Summerfield*,
for instance, is where Stock were driven up for the Summer Months
and where there was presumably a Shieling or Summer Hut, while
Shotley Field is such an Expanse near the Scotsman's Clearing. *Mor-
rowfield* must have been called after the Marsh that drained into the
neighbouring stream, just as *Morralee* signifies a Marshy Clearing.
(*Morralhirst*, on the other hand, denotes a Wood on a Gentle Slope).
High Field and *Field Head*, probably connected with Town Fields, are
self explanatory and *Durhamfield* was so called either because it was
owned by, or paid Tithe to, the Monastery of Durham. *Orchard Field*
does not appear to be the most suitable place for growing fruit but
it is not easy to suggest a better explanation. Certainly the Old English word 'orceard' has been known ever since the ninth century, if
not earlier. Before this there was in use a very similar Celtic word
denoting a Wood so it is quite possible that the farm has been named
after a much older place name.

The South East, however, is not the only part of the county where
these 'field' names are to be found, even if they happen to be particularly numerous there. When the old Palace of the Northumbrian
kings at Yeavering was vacated, a new one was built at Melmin, now
known as *Milfield*, the Expanse where there was probably to be found
a Cross or some kind of monument.

When corn was damaged by disease, it used to be known as 'slain',
and this is the explanation of *Slainsfield*, the Expanse where the
crops were Blighted in some way. Finally, there is *Yatesfield* which,
from the fact that it is in Redesdale, is unlikely to have belonged to
Eata, Bishop of Lindisfarne and later of Hexham, but probably to a
namesake of his.

NOTES

[16] maggots in the churn?
[17] Perhaps this was the same Dunn, whoever he was, who is reputed to have 'won
a battle against great odds' at Dunsmoor nearby.

CHAPTER 22

O F all the industries of Northumberland the Lead Industry must have been one of the oldest, for it is known that the Romans concerned themselves with it. Except for the Dark Ages which followed their retirement from the scene, men continued to mine lead for nearly two thousand years on Alston Moor and near the upper reaches of the East and West Allen. By the beginning of the nineteenth century there had come into being a settled pattern for dealing with it, which worked somewhat as follows:

Ore from Alston Moor was brought to the Smelt Mills at Whitfield, one of the principal ones being at *Cupola* which takes its name from the Cupola type of 'reverberatory' furnace. The coal required for smelting was brought from the Wood where Collan, the provost of Hexhamshire, had once lived, now known as *Coanwood*.

From Stublick Colliery came the coal that fed the furnace of the *Allen Mill* near *Allendale Town*, places which are called, of course, after the river of that name, originally known as the Alwent. Like the Alwin that gave its name to the Homestead of *Alwinton* this is a 'river-name' that seems to have been in common use among the Celts.

The raw material for this mill came from *Coalcleugh*, the 'highest village in England' which takes its name from the cheap and nasty 'Crow' Coal that was mined there. Ore from Coalcleugh, as well as that from the district of the Nine Hills (in other words *Ninebanks*) and from the Hills in which the East Allen rises (*Allenheads*) was also fed to the various Smelt Mills of Hexhamshire such as *Dukesfield*.

It used to be thought that the name of this place originated with the activities of the Duke of Somerset after the battle of Hexham

Levels not far away, but in fact it describes the Open Expanse where Ducca lived. It is just possible that *Dukershag*, near Prudhoe, owes its name to a settler of the same ilk. In 1434 the place is described as Deuffenbourne, which may have represented the Stream by Ducca's Fen or Marsh, whereas the modern name would refer to the Dry Peat in that Marsh.

Another of these mills in the Shire, or rather its Refining Chamber, is commemorated by the name *Finechambers Mill* and yet another by *Smelting Syke*. The Little Stream in question was presumably the source of power for the mill and it brings to mind the delightfully named *Sunday Sight* near Bellingham. In 1325 the name was Sunday-heugh or Sundayheigh. If the former is correct the name would presumably stand for the Spur of a Hill that was 'sundered', Set Apart or Private. This does not make very much sense but if 'heigh' is correct, the meaning is an Enclosure, but the language Scandinavian, which is unlikely but perfectly possible. Subsequently the place was known as Sunday Burn and (one supposes) Sunday Sike until, in 1663, it blossomed forth as Sunday Sight, the Little Stream 'far from the madding crowd'.

The coal to fire these furnaces in the Shire came all the way from *Greymare Hill* near Whittonstall which, like *Graymare* near Belford, takes its name from a Boundary Mark in the form of a Grey stone; in this case the Standestone or Standing Stone. The Peathouse that still exists at Allenheads is a reminder of earlier days when the fuel used for smelting the Lead came not from coal diggings but from the Peatmosses, along tracks such as are commemorated by *Peatgate*. Names like Hag Hill and Hag Bank denote places from which yet another fuel was brought, in the shape of wood.

The working conditions both in the mines and the smelt mills must have been primitive at best, and insufferably dangerous at worst. The fumes from the mills, for example, were so noxious that they had to be carried away in flues built underground and culminating in the tall chimneys which are still a feature of the landscape. The twin flues from the Allen Mill totalled nearly five miles in length and enabled, by condensation, appreciable quantities of lead to be recovered. A good deal of the stone for their construction was quarried at *Frolar Meadows* (sometimes known as Frawler Meadows), a farm that owes its name to the family of Frawler, a representative of which, John Ferroler, was to be found at Whitfield as lately as 1552.

When one considers the bulk of the ore and the weight of the lead that it yielded, it must be obvious that transport was a major headache, particularly as, until 1826, there were no roads whatever in the Allendales. Over the moors then, by tracks known, from the ponies that traversed them, as Galloway Roads, went the ore to the smelt mills. A 'Newcastle Fother' of just over a ton was divided between nine ponies and the whole pack train, amounting to anything from twelve to twenty animals, each with a man or boy leading it, must have been a common sight winding its leisurely way over the moors. Considering the quantity of ore that was required to produce a comparatively small amount of lead and the method of transporting it which, incidentally, cost twice as much in winter as it did during the rest of the year, it is remarkable that anyone could afford to mine or deal in the stuff at all.

No wonder also that the parties chiefly interested, that is to say the Beaumont family and the London Lead Company, were anxious to improve the road situation. Indeed they joined forces early in the nineteenth century to construct a road down East Allendale which would join up with the projected canal which was to run from Carlisle to Newcastle. At about the same time Greenwich Hospital, to whom the Derwentwater Estates had been awarded, and who therefore had a direct interest in the Lead mines, financed another road from Alston Moor to the mill at Langley.

From the mills, the next problem was to move the lead to Stella, on the Durham bank of the Tyne, whence it could be shipped to London and thence as far afield as India and China, for it was one of the most remunerative forms of outward cargo that the East India Company handled. The name *Stella* denotes a Clearing with a Sheepfold in it and the same Northumbrian word 'stell', or 'stelling', appears again in *Stell Green* and in *The Stelling*. In other parts of the county the same kind of circular stone enclosure is known as 'stank', which should on no account, and even in the wettest weather, be confused with that Old English word which denotes a fish-pond or stagnant ditch.

In fact, the journey to the Tyne was made in carts by way of the

Lead Road that started at Sparty Lea, the drivers staying the night
at the Inn at *Leadhill* where the Lead Road crosses Watling Street.
This same Road (or Gate) provides the explanation of *Leadgate* near
Whitfield and *Leadgate* near Whittonstall (unlike the place in
Durham that takes its name from a 'hlid-geat' or Swing-gate).

A curiously named farm, not far from this road, is *Litherage*. In
the sixteenth century it appears as Litterigem, and sometime later as
Little Ragg, but the name must surely have originated in Litharge,
the technical name for Oxydised Lead after the Silver has been
extracted.

A name that has no possible connection with the Lead Industry is
Leadpipe Hall, near Lowick. As in the case of *Lightpipe Hall*, it
seems highly probable that the old English 'lytel' has lost its 'l', as is
fairly common, and that the meaning is, in each case, a Little Watercourse.

The Coal Industry in Northumberland which, of course, became
immeasurably more important, was also carried on in Roman times.
It began again in the latter half of the thirteenth century with the
exploitation of the seams that reach the surface along the north side
of the Tyne valley.

In medieval times coal seems, right from the beginning, to have
been in the hands of the Church, and it was the monks of Tynemouth Priory who first began to work it. By 1530, they were leasing
the pits near Aelfsige's Farm—in other words *Elswick*—to others
and sending away considerable quantities, most of it to London.
This coal, known as 'sea coal' because the sea was the only practical
method of transport, was beginning as early as the fourteenth century to change the habits of the richer Londoners, who were rapidly
replacing their thatched roofs by red tiles in order to reduce the
consequent danger of fire. When Elizabeth I came to the throne,
the coalfields of Northumberland and Durham were still supplying
one third of the requirements of the whole country; a figure that
gradually reduced with time.

Until the monasteries were dissolved in the reign of Henry VIII,
the Coal trade continued to be almost a monopoly of the Church so
that, when nationalisation came about, one seventh of all coal

royalties still accrued to the Church Commissioners.

When deriving the names of places connected with Coal, one has to take some care to differentiate the real thing, as it were, from the Charcoal that used to be burnt in such large quantities, and which was used for smelting iron until the discovery was finally made which enabled it to be done with Coal.

Coalcleugh we have already looked at. *Coaly Hill* near Westerhope and almost all the farms called *Coal Houses* are certainly connected with Coal. Shallow holes or Pits from which to dig Coal gave *Colpitts* (once Colpottes) its name, and deeper ones explain *Pitland Hills* near Birtley.

The collieries themselves acquired a variety of names, often connected with the people who had sunk them, or of their wives or daughters, such as Montague, Maria and Isabella. The Napoleonic wars were responsible for a crop of colliery names such as Wellington and Duke, and also *Nelson* and *Blucher* which have both given their name to villages. *Percy Main* takes its name from one of the pits like Bigges Main and Lawson Main, that worked the High Main seam of coal just north of the Tyne. *Rising Sun Farm* is called after the Pit of that name near Wallsend. *Brunswick* is the rather uninspiring name given to what was, until recently, known as Dinnington Colliery.

Then there are two villages, at least, which are named after the families who used to own the coal royalties. At *Radcliffe* the land belonged to the Derwentwater family, whose name in turn originated from a Red Cliff, and the village itself sprang from the miners' cottages required for the working of the coal there.

The case of *Hazlerigg* is not so simple. The family of Hazelrig, Hazlerigge (or whatever spelling you may prefer) seems to have been called after the place of that name near Chatton; the meaning being, quite literally, the Ridge where Hazels grew. There was also a branch, however, at Eslington who owned land in the South East of the county. Simon of Hazlerigg, for instance, was valet to Edward I and is described in 1281 as Lord of Weetslade and West Brunton.

Sir Arthur Hazelrig was one of the commissioners at the trial of Charles I, though he did not sign the death warrant. Having been appointed Parliamentary Commissioner in the North, he came into possession of so much land that had previously been in the hands of the Church as to earn him the nickname of 'Bishop of Durham'. In 1818 another Sir Arthur of that ilk obtained a royal licence (mercifully for us) to regularise the spelling of the family name which had, long before this, been given to a village near Cramlington. Subsequently the place acquired the name of *Camperdown*.

Some time after 1860 the name of Hazlerigg was given to the colliery village that sprang up near Dinnington. Strangely enough the land about here no longer belonged to the Hazleriggs, the last of the Northumberland property having been sold to Matthew Bell and others in 1763.

Finally there are two or three names, at least, which are connected with the Coal trade but rather more indirectly. One is *Peck's Houses* near Kenton, named after Richard Peck who was a noted 'viewer' or mining engineer of the eighteenth century and developed a great number of those shallow mines whose spoil still pockmarks the landscape to the west of Newcastle. *Peck Riding*, however, is something quite different: it means the Clearing on the Pike, or Peak, of the hill. Another place, curiously enough, is *Bullocksteads*, also near Kenton and once described as Bullitt's Steads, but is thought to have taken its name from John Bullock, one of Richard Peck's associates.

A third is Killingworth, of imperishable memory, for here it was that George Stephenson lived and worked when he invented Blucher, his very first locomotive, and tried him out on the waggon way of the colliery there. 'Seein' is believin'. sor' he used to say, 'Howway to Killingworth and se what maa Blucher can dee'.

The name *Killingworth* is one of a strictly limited number in Northumberland that incorporate the Old English 'worth', meaning the Enclosure round a Homestead, or even the Homestead itself. In this case it was Cylla's People who gave the place its name. At *Backworth* it was Bacca and at *Pegswood* (once Peggesworth and Pegiz' Town) a gentleman called Pecg. Another place with the same kind of origin is *Aldworth*—the Old Homestead.

CHAPTER 23

A<small>N</small> account given by a traveller passing through Northumberland early in the eighteenth century falls unflatteringly on our ears, though perhaps the county may not at that time have been worse than many others. 'The greater part of the cottages' it ran 'are of stone or sod covered with rushes or turf but principally a clay daubing and thatched scarcely the height of a man'. It goes on to say that 'it is not uncommon to see men of rank on horse-back with a fresh turf for saddle and twisted straw for girths'. Farmers are described as carrying manure to their fields in creels, or panniers, balanced behind them on their horse's back. On reaching the field, two pins were released and the contents dropped where required: if one pin was removed before the other, the creel would swing round and knock the operator off his horse. This may appear fairly primitive to us now, but at least it shows an improvement on the Westmorland method which entailed the womenfolk carrying the creels on their backs.

By the beginning of the nineteenth century the Industrial Revolution, though ruining the appearance of Tyneside, had brought the North Country into much closer touch with the outside world. The trains of pack-horses were no longer to be seen in most parts of Northumberland after about 1830, any more than they were in other parts of England, and better roads and easier travel meant that the less accessible parts of the county could come more into line with the rest. Yet Hodgson, describing Corbridge at the same date (round about the time of Queen Victoria's accession) was not very appreciative, though one would hardly call the place inaccessible. Certainly the Scots had found it easy enough for they sacked it three times in the first half of the fourteenth century alone. Perhaps the hopelessness of rebuilding one's house in the certain knowledge that it would soon be demolished once more, laid a blight upon the place which persisted into later centuries. Or, of course, it may have been more typical of the county than one cares to consider.

'The town (for such its antiquity demands that it be styled) is dirty' wrote Hodgson, 'and in all the streets except that through which the Newcastle and Carlisle road passes, is filthy with middens and pigstyes, with railings before them of split board etc. The population seem half-fed; the women sallow, thin armed, and the men flabby, potbellied and tenderfooted; but still the place bears the appearance of being ancient'. There speaks the antiquarian that Roger North (when writing about Bywell) said was in us all.

Whatever the nature of such 'towns', the later eighteenth and early nineteenth centuries saw very considerable advances in agriculture, and farm steadings were being rebuilt all over the county. The profits of trade, and particularly of coal and lead mining and of shipbuilding, were ploughed back into the land; swamps were drained and farms created.

Names had to be found for these new creations and every sort of imaginative (and unimaginative) title came into being: the great difficulty now is to distinguish the old from the new, the corruptions from the originals. Take for instance *The Trinket* for which there seems no sensible explanation. *The Grips*, however, is clearly definable for (like Gilchester) it contains our word for a channel and therefore means The Ditches, or something of the sort.

To pingle means, to a Tynesider at any rate, to work away at something without achieving very much. There was, indeed, an old expression used when one was not anxious to pay for someone else, telling him to 'gan pingle in y'r ain poke neuk', that is to say, 'fish around in the corner of your own pocket'. It comes as something of an anti-climax to find that *The Pingle* is Old English for a Small Enclosure, so that the name may well be very ancient. The same applies to *The Gusset* which is an accurate description of the narrow, triangular shape of the original farm.

The Lamparts has caused a good deal of heart-searching so far as its derivation is concerned and, again, is of pretty ancient origin. In 1291 it was known as Lythel (little) Lampard, but in 1583 The

Lampert. One of our foremost experts on place names has described it as 'clearly not of English origin'. When one considers, however, that a Clay (or Loam) Pit used to be known by our ancestors as a Lam-pytt, the explanation becomes obvious—it is the place of the Clay Pits.

The Boat Farm at Bellingham is easily explained by the fact that a Ferryboat used to be moored there but *Longboat*, near Longhough-ton, almost certainly derives its name from the same word that in-spired Bought Hill. In other words it must have been the 'lang bucht' or Long Byre where the Ewes were milked in winter. *The Brig* is also, of course, nothing to do with the sea: it describes, in fact, the Bridge which carried one of the old Drove Roads from Scotland over what is now called the Brig burn. Neither have *Black Carts* and *Green Carts* any connection with horses for they take their names from the Rocky Moor (or 'ceart'), one part of which is Heather-clad, or black, and the other Grassy and therefore green.

The Rift, also, has quite a respectable ancestry for it takes its name from a stream that in 1290 was known as the Rysedeneburne, from the Rushy Valley through which it flowed, while *The Rink* describes a Ring: probably of Stones. *The Haining* has borne the same name since 1304, and probably long before that. The expression 'to hain', meaning to enclose or preserve grass from being eaten by stock so that it can (for instance) be made into hay, is still in everyday use on Northumbrian farms. Originally the word just meant an Enclosure, which was probably used to keep cattle in rather than out, and this is also the meaning in *Haining Hall* and *Haining Rigg*.

When the Earl of Surrey was on his way north on the march which was to culminate so successfully in the Battle of Flodden, he camped at Bolton, near Alnwick, with 26,000 men. Requiring a parley, James IV of Scotland sent his herald Islay with a message. The latter, however, was detained by the English 'at a village called Mylo ... untyll the coming there of the sayde earle'. And so *The Mile*, near Glanton, enters history, and with it *Mile End*. The names are a little confusing because the former is one mile from Glanton and the latter one mile from Eslington. It seems most unlikely that the Scottish herald was in any way connected with *Islay Hall*, near Belford which probably represents Gisla's Law, or Hill.

The Tythe Barn, in Allendale, and *Tithe Hill*, near Cornhill, were no doubt places where Tithe was brought when it was customary to pay it in kind. Neither *Seatsides* nor *High Seat* have anything to do with seats in the modern sense of the word. The first is a Hillside where there was a Roman camp and the second near a Roman mile-castle: in each case the ancient walls would have provided excellent shelter for cattle or sheep and explain why both are named after Cattle Folds. *Loudside*, once known as Laudside, may denote a Hillside that belonged to the Lord of the manor or was allotted to him when the common was enclosed.

Throughout medieval and Tudor times 'enclosure' of land in some form or other had been going on. Fresh clearings had been made and fields won from forest and moor, and enclosed with earthworks, hedges or walls to increase the Town fields. This was followed in many cases by the enclosure, by mutual consent of the villagers, of portions of the waste which formed an integral part of the system. At the same time the individual farms which were so much more common in Northumberland than elsewhere, had been reclaiming more and more virgin land and fencing it in, so that names like *Intake, Intack Head* and *The Winning* entered upon the scene.

In other parts of England, however, a different kind of enclosure had begun which was accelerated by the shortage of labour that had been created by the Black Death in the fourteenth century. When there were no longer enough villein farmers left alive to till the land properly, the only way in which the Lord of the Manor could ensure its continued cultivation was, as we should now put it, to rationalise his holdings. This he tried to do by putting an end to the wasteful practice of cultivating different little strips of land all over the place, and by 'taking the land in hand' and working it himself as a block with paid labour. Sometimes the town fields were rearranged into a smaller number of hedged enclosures; sometimes, as the production of wool became increasingly remunerative, into sheep pasture. On occasion this was done with the consent of those who farmed the land: more often it was not. Still more serious was the wholesale enclosure by the Lord of the Manor of the waste which should have been common to the villagers and without which the town field system could not operate properly. The outcry which resulted from such enclosures is exemplified by the eighteenth-century rhyme:

The law doth punish man or woman
That steals the goose from off the common,
But lets the greater felon loose
That steals the common from the goose.

In Northumberland, difficulties due to enclosure were much less than elsewhere; partly because of the smaller proportion of land held in common and partly because a great deal was done by agreement. As has already been suggested, the creation of embankments and hedges which resulted from carving up the great thousand acre fields, was also a useful deterrent to the Scots. The reduction of the number of individual holdings, however, was by no means so desirable for 'in an area where a holding means not only a piece of land that grows wheat and feeds sheep but a horseman in harness, the dropping out of a holding or its merging with that of someone else results in the weakening of the force on which the peace of the border depends'.

Opinions regarding the desirability or otherwise of enclosure varied considerably, and so we find the tenants of High Buston using the depredations of the Scots to strengthen their petition for enclosure, while those of Hartley and Seaton Delaval wanted exactly the reverse. They complained indeed that the Lord of the Manor was buying out the freeholders and evicting the tenants, pulling down their houses and farming the land with hired labour.

With the end of border warfare on the grand scale, agricultural improvements of all sorts proceeded merrily, enclosure taking place by private arrangement not only with the villagers but between neighbouring Landlords. It was made all the easier by the change in the status of tenants, enabling them to pay rents in cash rather than in boon-days (or dargues) and other forms of service to the Lord of the Manor. This was followed by the division of many townships not, at first, into a number of separate farms but into halves, thirds and quarters so that enclosure could continue piecemeal and without undue hardship. Thus in 1833 the Township of Bellingham was divided into Charlton East Quarter, Charlton West Quarter, Hesleyside Quarter, Lee Mailing Quarter, Nook Quarter and Tarsetburn

Quarter. This kind of subdivision also, of course, explains such titles as Kelly Quarter, Hexhamshire High Quarter and Shotley High Quarter which we have already encountered, and probably the six Grieveships of Allendale as well.

When, around 1729 it became fashionable to introduce Private Bills into Parliament under which enclosures could be properly and fairly organised, the requirement for them in Northumberland was inconsiderable for a great deal had already been done. Nevertheless, between about that date and 1860, a number of Enclosure Acts affecting the county were passed through Parliament, the first of these Acts affecting Elsdon in 1729 and one of the last concerning Halt-whistle in 1844. After this there were only a few sporadic Acts such as that of 1853 enclosing Hareshaw Common and that of 1859 concerning the drainage and subsequent enclosure of Prestwick Carr.

When the land was re-divided after an Enclosure the allocation was sometimes made by drawing lots, so that a name appears like *Lord's Lot*, denoting the share that went to the Lord of the Manor. An even clearer instance is *Cavil Head*, for the word 'cavil', used particularly in the Pits, actually signifies a Lot or Share. It should not be imagined, however, that *Bonas Hill* has anything to do with such a division of spoils. It is called after a Charnel or Bone House.

If the new farm was largely composed of one particular town field, it might be christened *Southfield Blue House*, *Crookham East Field*, *Inland Pastures* or *Far Pasture*. If it contained or marched with what had originally been Demesne land it might, if not called *Snitter Demesne* or the like, take a name such as *Old Town* (as at Otterburn) or *Lesbury Town Foot* (once known as Hunger-up). *Clipper Head-land*, like *Warksfieldhead* presumably owes its name to the Headland of the original Town field (where Sheep were Clipped) while names like *The Reins* and *The Reenes* are a reminder of the Waterfurrows that separated the strips of arable land or the slopes between strips that had been terraced.

Or the farm might be named after the recipient; hence *Temperley Grange*, *Noble Lands* (already known in 1626) and *Benson's Fell*. It might be thought that *Frenches Close*, near Prudhoe, could be explained in somewhat the same way as Frenchman's Row at Throckley which, originally built for pitmen at the new collieries nearby, was used to house French priests who fled from the Revolution. In fact history records as early as 1650 a William French of Frenches Close whose family must have been the beneficiaries of an early enclosure. *The Crescent Farm* is called after the shape of its Plantation while *Bays Leap* took its name from a little crag over which a fugitive jumped his horse and was killed.

Wager House really is connected with a Wager and perhaps *Bogle Houses* really had a Haunt. Certainly *Land Ends*, near Haydon Bridge used to harbour a bogle called Josse. On occasion he was known to be malicious but, on the whole, did more good than harm for he 'frequently assisted servants in foddering the horses and often at night the hayracks would be crammed with hay ... In the morning after the men had watered, foddered and dressed horses and had gone in to get breakfast, Josse would put the horses in full harness ready for cart or plough accordingly as they were wanted'. Land Ends and, incidentally, *World's End*, probably commemorate Fields that were particularly remote from the 'town', or may even describe cultivation strips that happen to lie at the far end of such fields.

Sionside, one supposes, took its name, like the Duke of Northumberland's Syon House, from the Biblical Sion; neither *Paradise* nor *Seldom Seen* need any comment but *Frolic* surely does. Is this another corruption; was it created for a joke, or is the name intended just to suggest Gladness?

Dancing Hill near Belford used to be known as Gay Hill and this use of 'dancing' for Joyful (as in Scotland) is probably the explanation also of *Dancing Hall*. This place was a well known playground for the Northumberland Fairies, whose queen lived on Fawdon Hill and whose burial ground is, or was, to be seen in the grounds of Brinkburn Priory. Perhaps *Shining Hall* has the same kind of meaning. Alternatively the name may have something to do with a Spectre. Certainly *Elf Hills* is a reminder of the days when Goblins and fairies frequented the countryside and Elf Shots, that is to say stone arrowheads, could be picked up to prove it. There was even a Green place where they collected and which, in consequence, was known as Elfa, or Of the Elves, and now as *Elpha Green*.

Scarlet Hall was probably Scarlet Hill, or the Hill with the Steep

Clearing. *Maidens Hall* (once Face-the-Deil) is one of those names like Maiden Castle and Maidens' Causeway, the literal meaning of which is obvious but any sensible explanation singularly lacking. Was the place inhabited by Maiden Ladies? Was it originally a Hill so easily defensible that Girls could have held it against all comers? Were Nuns involved? One simply does not know.

Another mystery is why anyone should want to call their farm *Hotch Pudding* (late Hog's Pudding and, before that, Pigs Hall), *Plum Pudding* or *Dumpling Hall*. On the other hand *The Whiggs* has a perfectly rational explanation. When the freeholders of Matfen bought a farm, the rent from which was to support a Non-conformist Chapel, it was at a time when all Dissenters were known as Whigs. Another name that is quite understandable is *Temperance*.

When the shepherd's house at Town O' Rule, in Berwickshire, was built in the year of Waterloo the owner, being a strict teetotaller, would not allow the masons to drink at work, with the result that the locals christened it *Drythropple*. It used to be the custom in Northumberland to give the masons and carpenters 'couple beer' in the form of ale or spirits when the first couple of a house was hoisted, and there seems little doubt that, in the case of Drythropple, this custom was neglected.

On the reverse of the coin are the farms called after Public Houses. *The Black Swine, The Lion Farm, The Three Tuns, The Seven Stars, The Swan Farm* and the rest of them. And, of course, *Twice Brewed*. The original inn, known earlier as The Twice Brewed Ale, was where *East Twice Brewed Farm* now stands.

At first sight there would seem little to connect *Iron-Sign*, near Harlow Hill, with the saying 'Good wine needs no bush' but there is in fact a connection. There once stood there an inn built, like all too many houses along the line of the Wall, from Roman stone. Instead of displaying the traditional 'bush' commemorating the Ivy plant sacred to Bacchus, the tavern sported an innovation in the shape of an Iron Sign.

There are no traces now of an inn at *Way-to-Wooler*, whose name is presumably connected with the Belford Road; or at *Biteabout*, despite the possible affinity that its name bears to Bide-a-bit: a map of 1828 shows it as Biter Bit! Or, indeed, at *Tarry*, near Eglingham, the meaning of which remains a mystery, though it seems possible that the name derives from the Cleft Spur of a Hill.

Kitty Brewster, on the other hand, traditionally takes its name from an Alehouse where Kitty the Brewster brewed her ale. No doubt, like other ale-wives, she was subject to a simple and effective test that used to be carried out by the village ale-tester or constable, in order to ensure that the liquor was up to standard. He used to don a pair of leather breeches and, appearing in the ale-house without warning, ask for a glass of ale. He would then pour a little of it on the bench and sit down in it, drinking on and off but never stirring from the bench. After exactly half-an-hour he would get up, in which case all was well. But if he stuck to the bench it meant that the ale had been adulterated with sugar, and woe betide Kitty, or any other Brewster, who was caught out.

Another possible explanation has been advanced, namely that Kitty Brewster is a corruption of two Celtic words meaning a Steep, Wooded Slope. This seems a little far fetched in this case; particularly as the farm was originally known as Buck's Hill.

Union Hall must surely have been named in celebration of the Act of Union with Scotland. If it had only been situated just a little nearer to Newcastle it might have provided the farmyard through which John Wesley's horses galloped after running away with his carriage down Denton Bank. *Albion House, Wae's Me* and *Royalty* are presumably pure fancy but *Dam House* takes its name from a Mill Dam or Dammed Pond, just as *Dam Dykes* is called after the Pond that fed the ornamental lake at Arcot.

There are a number of places known as *Close House*; presumably because of Land Enclosed there. The farm near Heddon-on-the-Wall was once known as the Abbey Close but had nothing to do with the Church, being a corruption of Albery Close. Yet *Close House* near Simonburn, once part of Hallbarns, was occupied in 1683 by Dorothy Close, which seems more than a coincidence. Perhaps *The Doll's House* is descriptive of the appearance of a building in the same way that a certain lodge in the county seems to be generally known as the Inkpot.

Surely the strangest method of all for naming a new farm is to call it after a battle. It seems just conceivable that one might want to

call a place *Waterloo*, but why *Bomarsund*, after an obscure engage-
ment in the Crimean War, and why *Pondicherry?* Dunkirk we have
encountered previously, as well as Camperdown near Cramlington,
but *Camperdown* near Shotley presents a real difficulty. As lately as
1844 the farm was known as Pike Hill, meaning the Pointed Hill.
Why its name was subsequently changed, half a century after Duncan's victory over the Dutch, remains a mystery. *Havannah* has
appeared more than once and presumably has something to do with
one of the Spanish wars in which the West Indies were concerned.
Botany, of course, has no connection with a battle but it is even more
difficult to understand then if it had, for the name of a Penal Settlement does not, one would think, provide a very attractive title for a
farm. *Canada, Nova Scotia* and *New York* seem to our ears equally
uninspired.

Dilkusha Hall is one of those apparently fancy names which must
surely have special associations, as in the case of *Boca Chica*. This is
called after an island, or Cay, off the coast of Florida and the name is
thought to have been used by an eighteenth-century sea captain to
describe the farm in which he settled down, a 'sailor home from the
sea'.

So much for the names of places and farms that have been, or
might appear to have been, named during the last couple of hundred
years. They form just another chapter in a story which, it is hoped,
has done something to show how the evolution of this, the most
English of counties, can be traced simply by a proper understanding
of the names of its towns, villages and farms.

BIBLIOGRAPHY

Among the sources consulted were the following:—

Allgood Papers, The (Nunwick).

Antiquaries, Society of, Newcastle. *Archaeologia Aeliana* (84 vols). *Archaeologia Transactions* (33 vols).

Armstrong, Lt. A. and Son. *A Map of the County of Northumberland*, 1769.

Armstrong and others. *The Place Names of Cumberland*, 1952.

Banks, H. R. *The Scottish Border Country.*

Bailey and Culley. *General View of the Agriculture of Northumberland*, 1805.

Bain, J. (Ed.). *The Border Papers 1560-1603.* 1894-6.

Balfour, M. C. *Examples of Printed Folk-lore concerning Northumberland*, 1904.

Bates, C. J. *The Border Holds of Northumberland*, 1891.

Bean, J. M. W. *The Estates of the Percy Family 1416-1537.* 1958.

Bede, The Venerable. *Ecclesiastical History of the British Nation.*

Bell Family, Surveyors, Portfolios of Plans and Papers.

Berwickshire Naturalists Club, History of the (34 vols).

Blackett Papers, The (Matfen).

Brockett, J. T. *A Glossary of North Country Words*, 1846.

Brown, A. *Dictionary of the Scottish Language*, 1845.

Bruce & Stokoe. *The Border Minstrelsy*, 1965.

Butlin, R. A. *Northumberland Field Systems*, reprinted from the Agricultural History Review Vol. XII, 1964.

Bradley, A. G. *The Romance of Northumberland*, 1908.

Camden. *Britannia.* Edition of 1695.

Cameron, K. *English Place Names.*

Carlisle, Bishop of. *Border Laws*, 1747.

Charlton, Dr E. *Memorials of North Tyndale and its four surnames*, 1871.

Copley, G. J. *English Place names and their origin*, 1968.

Cox. *Magna Britannia—Northumberland*, 1720.

Delaval Papers, Some of the

Dickson. *The Wards, Divisions, Parishes and Townships of Northumberland*, 1833.

Dixon, D. Dippie. *Upper Coquetdale*, 1903.
Whittingham Vale, 1895.

Dixon, Hubert. *An Allendale Miscellany.*

Dixon, S. F. *History of the Saxon Royal Town of Corbridge-on-Tyne*, 1912.

Ekwall, E. *The Concise Oxford Dictionary of English Place Names* 4th Ed., 1960.

Enclosure Maps, Various.

Estate Maps, Various.

Fraser, C. M. (Ed.) *The Northumberland Lay Subsidy Roll of 1296*, 1968.

Gauld, H. D. *Brave Borderland.*

Greenwood, C. and I. *Map of the County of Northumberland*, 1827.

Guppy, H. B. *The Homes of Family Names*, 1890.

Harbottle, Rental Roll of the Lordship of

Headlam, Sir C. (Ed.). *The Three Northern Counties*, 1939.

Heslop, R. O. *Northumberland Words*, 1892.

Hodgkin and others. *Northumbria.* Lectures delivered to the Literary & Philosophical Society, 1898.

Hodgson, Rev. John. *An account of the Parish of Hartburn.*
History of Northumberland, 1863. (7 Vols).
Inedited contributions to the History of Northumberland.

Hone, N. J. *The Manor and Manorial Records*, 1906.

Hoskins, W. G. *Fieldwork in Local History*, 1967.
The Making of the English Landscape, 5th Imp., 1963.

Hughes, E. *North Country Life in the 18th Century, The North East 1700-1750*, 1952.

King's England Series (Ed. A. Mee). *Northumberland.*

Lang, J. *A Land of Romance*, 1930.

Lee, W. *Historical Notes of Haydon Bridge and District*, 1876.

Leland. *Itinerary in England & Wales (1535-43)* Ed. L Toulmin Smith.

Loraine of Kirkharle, Pedigree and Memoirs of, 1902.

McAndrews, J. *Amble and District*, 1909.

Mack, J. L. *The Border Line*, 1926.

Mackenzie, E. *A View of the County of Northumberland*, 1825.

Mawer, A. *The Place Names of Northumberland and Durham*, 1920.

Middleton Papers, The (Belsay).

Northumberland County History Committee. *Northumberland County History* (15 Vols).

  Northumberland Quarter Sessions. *Ancient Indictments*, 1592-1630.

  Northumberland Quarter Sessions. *Order Book*, 1689-97.

  Northumberland, *A List of Wards, Divisions, Parishes and Constableries, Alnwick*, 1817.

Ogle, Sir Henry. *Ogle and Bothel*, 1902.

Ordnance Survey. *6 inches to the mile*, 1869.

  6 inches to the mile, 1957.

  1 inch to the mile, 1963.

Parish Registers, Transcripts for Berwick, Haydon Bridge, Kirknewton and Ponteland.

Pease, Howard. *The Lord Wardens of the Marches of England & Scotland*, 1913.

  Northumbria's Decameron, 1927.

Pevsner, N. *The Buildings of England, Northumberland*, 1957.

Reaney, P. H. *A Dictionary of British Surnames*, 1958.

Raine, Rev. J. *The History and Antiquities of North Durham*, 1852.

Raistrick and Jennings. *A History of Lead Mining in the Pennines*, 1965.

Richardson, M. A. *The Local Historian's Table Book*, 1846.

Ridley Papers, The (Blagdon).

Ridpath, George. *The Border History of England & Scotland—to the Union of the two crowns*, 1810.

Ridley, Nancy. *Portrait of Northumberland*, 1965.

Scott, J. *Berwick upon Tweed, History of the Town and Guild*, 1888.

Smith A. H. *English place-name Elements*, 1956.

  The Place names of Westmorland, 1967.

Sopwith. *An account of the Lead Mining districts of Alston Moor*, 1833.

Speed, J. *Map of Northumberland*, 1610.

Surtees Society. *The Priory of Hexham incl. The Black Book*. Ed. Rev J. Raine.

The Boldon Book. Ed. Rev. W. Greenwell.

The Brinkburn Chartulary. Ed. W. Page.

The Newminster Chartulary. Ed. Rev. J. T. Fowler.

Register of Estates of Roman Catholics in Northumberland.

Swinburne, Algernon. *Ballads of the English Border*, 1925.

Swinburne Papers, The (Capheaton).

Tate, G. *The History of the Borough, Castle and Barony of Alnwick*, 1866.

Thomson, Hugh. *Highways and Byways of Northumberland*, 1920.

Tithe Maps, Various.

Tomlinson, W. W. *Comprehensive Guide to the County of Northumberland*, 11th Ed., 1968.

Life in Northumberland during the 16th Century, 1897.

Trevelyan, G. M. *English Social History*, 1942.

Wallis, John. *The Natural History and Antiquities of Northumberland*, 1769.

INDEX

Valérie
81st birthday
present.